Creative
Gardening
with a
Computer
for the Older
Generation

Other Books of Interest

*****

Acknowledgements

The author and publishers would like to thank the following for their help:

GSP of Meadow Lane, St. Ives, Cambs., PE27 4LG, for their support and permission to reproduce screens from the Geoff Hamilton 3D Garden Designer and Plant Encyclopedia software and especially Joanna Brailsford, Marketing Communications Co-ordinator at GSP.

Also my wife Jill, for her forbearance and for sharing her gardening expertise during the preparation of this book.

Finally Geoff Hamilton, whose knowledge and expertise provided the basis for the software around which this book is written.

Creative Gardening with a Computer for the Older Generation

Jim Gatenby

BERNARD BABANI (publishing) LTD
The Grampians
Shepherds Bush Rd
London W6 7NF
England

www.babanibooks.com

Please Note

Although every care has been taken with the production of this book to ensure that any projects, designs, modifications and/or programs, etc., contained herewith, operate in a correct and safe manner and also that any components specified are normally available in Great Britain, the Publishers and Author do not accept responsibility in any way for the failure (including fault in design) of any project, design, modification or program to work correctly or to cause damage to any equipment that it may be connected to or used in conjunction with, or in respect of any other damage or injury that may be so caused, nor do the Publishers accept responsibility in any way for the failure to obtain specified components.

Notice is also given that if equipment that is still under warranty is modified in any way or used or connected with home-built equipment then that warranty may be void.

© 2004 BERNARD BABANI (publishing) LTD

First Published - February 2004

British Library Cataloguing in Publication Data:

A catalogue record for this book is available from the
British Library

ISBN 0 85934 603 X
Cover Design by Gregor Arthur
Printed and bound in Great Britain by Cox and Wyman Ltd

About this Book

This book aims to show that, with the right software, the computer is the perfect tool for designing and developing a garden and for providing comprehensive plant information.

The book is based on the inexpensive Geoff Hamilton 3D Garden Designer and Plant Encyclopedia; this software is easy to use - you don't need to be a computer expert to read this book or use the software. "Virtual" gardening on the computer allows you to maintain your gardening interest in comfort - even in the depths of winter.

This book should appeal to anyone who is curious about the way computers can be used in garden design and also to existing or potential users of garden design and plant information software. The book shows how the 3D Garden Designer software can be used to create a garden from a blank canvas, incorporating ready-made designs such as fences, water features, paths and patios, garden furniture and structures such as arbours and summerhouses. Plants and landscaping features can be edited and arranged in any shape including curves. Plant encyclopedias allow every characteristic, including care and maintenance, of thousands of plants, shrubs and trees to be researched to find the most suitable for your particular garden.

A 3-dimensional view allows you to "stroll" through the garden and check out the design from all angles. Then the design can easily be modified, if necessary, avoiding expensive and time-wasting gardening disasters.

A chapter is devoted to the excellent Geoff Hamilton Plant Encyclopedia (available separately) and appendices cover methods of dealing with sloping ground and explanations of essential computer jargon.

Readers of this book can buy the best-selling Geoff Hamilton software at half price - please see page 181 for details.

About the Author

Jim Gatenby trained as a Chartered Mechanical Engineer and initially worked at Rolls-Royce Ltd using computers in the analysis of jet engine performance. He obtained a Master of Philosophy degree in Mathematical Education by research at Loughborough University of Technology and taught mathematics and computing to 'A' Level for many years. His most recent posts included Head of Computer Studies and Information Technology Coordinator. During this time he has written many books in the fields of educational computing and Microsoft Windows.

The author has considerable experience of teaching students of all ages, in school and in adult education. For several years he successfully taught the well-established CLAIT course and also GCSE Computing and Information Technology. The author is himself a member of the over 50s club and an enthusiastic gardener.

Trademarks

Contents

1

Introduction

Why Use a Computer for Garden Design?

The idea of using a computer to assist with such a traditional activity as gardening may initially seem surprising. In fact, the planning of a new garden or the redesigning of an older one can be quite a complex task; a computer can greatly simplify the process. A huge library of ready-made high quality designs for common garden structures like fences and greenhouses is provided. Every conceivable surface from lawns to paths and paved areas, etc., is available at the touch of a button.

Plant encyclopedias available on Compact Disc provide excellent on-screen colour photographs and give complete details about thousands of flowers, shrubs and trees. After selection your plants can be placed on the design then moved to your favoured position.

During the winter months you can continue "virtual gardening" in comfort using your computer. You can create new garden designs or redesign existing areas, then take a "walk" through the virtual garden and see how it looks in 3 dimensions. Best of all you can experiment with lots of different designs and layouts on the screen, without producing a mountain of waste paper!

With a garden design program capable of displaying 3-dimensional views you should be able to avoid expensive and time-consuming mistakes in the real garden. Such errors might include small plants obscured by taller ones or groups of flowers whose colours clash. The overall appearance of a garden based on a carefully planned design should be more pleasing than a garden which has developed in a haphazard fashion. Using a computer-based plant encyclopedia should ensure that plants are selected which will thrive in a particular situation, taking into account local factors such as sun, shade and soil type.

The work in this book is based around Geoff Hamilton's 3D Garden Designer, the best-selling software incorporating the ideas of the much-loved television gardener.

Special Offer for Readers on Geoff Hamilton Software

Readers of this book can obtain the Geoff Hamilton 3D Garden Designer and Plant Encyclopedia software at half price. Please see pages 181 for details.

Currently there are three programs available in the Geoff Hamilton range of software, all supplied on CD-ROM. The basic program is the Garden Designer, for creating 2-dimensional garden plans, while the latest program is the 3D Garden Designer, currently on Version 3. Both of these Garden Design programs have their own built-in plant encyclopedia. In addition you can buy Geoff Hamilton's Plant Enclopedia, a stand-alone program providing comprehensive details of over 4000 plants. The plants are beautifully illustrated, showing the colours of flowers and foliage as they change throughout the year.

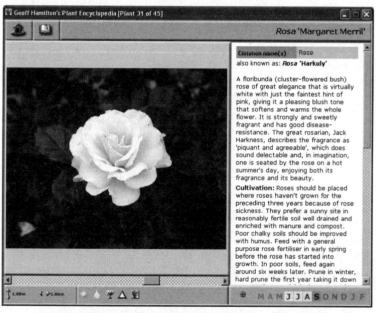

The plant encyclopedia can be searched by entering criteria such as Latin and Common names, plant type (annual, shrub or tree, etc.,) height and spread and local growing conditions including soil type, moisture and sunlight.

Computer Requirements

To utilize the Geoff Hamilton CDs you must have a PC-type computer. Fortunately most new computers currently on sale in the High Street, with the exception of the Apple Macintosh, conform to the PC standard. The computer must be fitted with a CD-ROM drive in order to install and run the software and it's also desirable to have a colour printer to make "hard copy" of your designs on paper.

In order to run software packages in general, a computer must meet certain technical requirements. These are usually listed on the outside of the packaging in which the new CD is supplied. For anyone not familiar with computers the technical requirements are likely to be incomprehensible and so they are not listed here.

However, if you have an older computer and wish to check its ability to run the Geoff Hamilton software, the minimum requirements are given in **Appendix 2** at the back of this book. Also included are explanations of the computer jargon and help with finding out the precise details for your particular computer. Fortunately any PC computer purchased in the last couple of years or so should be quite capable of running the software.

The Geoff Hamilton software is powerful yet reasonably priced and is available from the usual High Street computer suppliers and also by mail order. Technical support is available from GSP, at the following address:

GSP, Meadow Lane, St. Ives, Cambs, PE27 4LG

E-mail:support@gsp.cc   Web:www.gsp.cc

Please see page 181 for details of the special half price offer on Geoff Hamilton CDs for readers of this book.

The 3D Garden Designer - An Overview

In order to give you ideas and inspiration, the 3D Garden Designer CD includes samples of some of Geoff Hamilton's Town and Country Paradise Gardens, featured in the popular television programs from Barnsdale, as shown below.

Geoff Hamilton's
Town Paradise Garden

Clockwise from below:
Main planting; fountain planting; gazebo
and pond; conservatory; view from
gazebo (including fountain).

Several sample garden designs are provided on the CD, such as the one shown below in plan view.

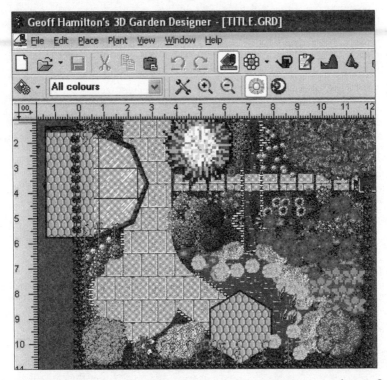

As shown above, the plan view can incorporate a variety of surfaces including lawns, paths and paved areas, and structures such as a greenhouse or an arbour. Creating a plan is discussed in more detail later in this book.

By clicking on any of the plants or trees as shown in the plan above, you can launch the built-in plant encyclopedia and find out complete details of the selected plant. You can also launch the **Care Calendar** which tells you how to look after the plants during the different months throughout the year, as shown by the extract on the next page.

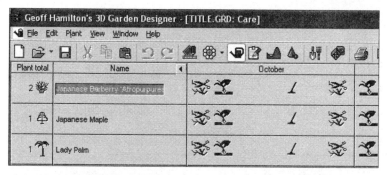

The Care Calendar and the various icons shown above (representing different maintenance tasks) are discussed in more detail later in this book.

A click of the mouse button converts the plan view shown on the previous page into a 3-dimensional view, enabling you to "walk" through the virtual garden and get an idea of what it will look like in real life.

"Cameras" placed at various locations in the garden enable you to see the design from lots of different viewpoints. Major changes to the design can easily be made on the screen and then permanently saved in the computer.

Inserting Surfaces and Structures

Using the 3D Garden Designer you can easily draw a basic 2-dimensional plan and add paths, paved areas, fences and walls, etc. These can be moved about, rotated and resized until you are happy with the layout. A large choice of surface and border materials is available, including the small samples shown below.

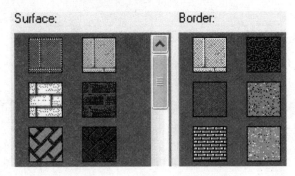

Common garden structures such as arbours, greenhouses, garages, ponds, etc., as well as outdoor lighting are available as high-quality artwork ready for immediately placing onto the plan. This artwork is far better than you could draw by hand and available at the click of a mouse button.

A variety of other objects which may be found in a garden such as cars, boats, animals and birds are also available as artwork to complete your design.

Editing, Saving and Printing a Design

A major advantage of any sort of computer-aided design is that changes can easily be made. There's no need to worry about making mistakes or trying out new ideas. Any part of a design can be deleted and redrawn on the screen. This is why computers have replaced the drawing board in so many situations. Garden structures such as greenhouses and arbours, paths and patios can be moved around, resized and rotated in the two-dimensional plan until you are happy with their position.

A design can be saved permanently on your computer's hard disc and printed out on paper in full colour. Several copies can be printed instantly. This would be useful, for example, if you wanted to discuss your requirements with gardening contractors or to show your design to family and friends. A design can be retrieved at a later time and major changes made if desired. You can even send a garden design to someone else as an attachment to an e-mail, via the telephone lines. (Saving, printing and e-mailing garden designs are discussed in detail later in this book.)

Plant Encyclopedias

Planting is obviously at the heart of all successful gardens and the plant encyclopedias built into programs such as Geoff Hamilton's 3D Garden Designer cover every detail of a plant, such as optimum soil types, preferred climate, Latin and Common names, height and width, flowering seasons and details of plant care and diseases.

It's even possible to view plants in their various colours throughout the year, by simply clicking the required month from a menu.

There are many more features in Geoff Hamilton's 3D Garden Designer and these are discussed in detail throughout the remainder of this book.

Design Considerations

The Existing Site

There may be a lot of site clearance work, for example to remove an old shed or unwanted trees and shrubs. One of our gardens required the removal of a large concrete area previously used as a shed base, before any actual gardening could begin. You may need to import a quantity of good top soil if your plot is full of builder's rubble or the soil is heavy clay. Another garden had a large area consisting of a foot depth of ash, accumulated from decades of coal fires. This had to be removed and replaced with top soil.

The Purpose of the Garden

You will need to form a clear idea of the type of garden you wish to create, by considering questions such as:

Will the garden be used primarily for relaxation, to sit in on long summer afternoons and evenings? This would suggest paved areas with seating and perhaps a barbecue, arbour or summer-house.

Remember, however, that a very small garden will look cluttered if there is too much garden furniture or too many built structures.

If children or grandchildren are likely to use the garden as a playground, lawns consisting of hard-wearing grass are essential. A pond would obviously be a bad idea if children will be playing unsupervised in the garden.

You might consider one or two focal points such as a statue or a gazebo to draw the eye, perhaps through an avenue of trees or shrubs. If you are trying to create an atmosphere for relaxation, then certain shapes such as circles and hexagons encourage you to rest a while, more so than long straight paths disappearing into the distance, for example. The following is one of the sample "virtual" gardens from Geoff Hamilton's 3D Garden Designer CD.

Gardening as a Hobby

Is the garden going to be one of your main hobbies, involving a lot of work like mowing, edging, pruning, raising seedlings, propagating cuttings and planting? Will you need a greenhouse, cold frames, compost bins and a vegetable plot?

Access for Disabled People

Care should be given in the design of paths and paved areas to allow easy wheelchair access. You would certainly need to avoid large steps, uneven surfaces and dangerous cambers and slopes. You might also include some raised beds, so that a disabled person can enjoy gardening without the need to bend down.

Encouraging Wildlife

The sight of birds and other wildlife in your garden can be a source of great pleasure to anyone, but particularly for older people who may not be very mobile. You don't need a large garden in the country to see wildlife; a small area in the town with a few trees and shrubs and some inexpensive feeders and bird boxes can receive visits from a colourful variety of birds, as well as squirrels, urban foxes and hedgehogs.

Care should be taken to ensure that birds have suitable "landing stages" near any feeders and bird boxes. These might be branches in adjacent trees or walls and fences. You might also consider placing small trees and shrubs in positions near the house so that birds and other wildlife can be seen by anyone confined to the house. Feeders and birdboxes should obviously be inaccessible to the usual garden predators.

Screening and Shelter

Depending on your situation, you may wish to erect screening in the form of fences, walls or fast-growing shrubs, to minimize the impact of neighbouring buildings or perhaps noise from a nearby motorway. Or you might want to screen off part of your garden as a utility area, to contain less aesthetic items such as a wheelie bin, clothes drier, compost bin, incinerator and fuel store. In our garden a large tank is used to store propane gas, since mains piped gas is not available in the locality. The gas tank has now  been partially screened using fencing and shrubs which should eventually provide complete screening.

If you live in an exposed situation you might need to provide shelter from the prevailing wind, to protect plants and shield the seating areas.

Maintenance Issues

If you don't want to spend a lot of time weeding, etc., low maintenance ground-cover plants, shrubs and trees should be considered. If you are retired, you may need to make lifestyle choices - do you want to spend a lot of time gardening? Alternatively would you rather have a low maintenance garden which will leave you free to do other things such as travelling, social activities or sport perhaps? If you are planning for the long term, bear in mind that as years go by you may find it harder to manage a large, high maintenance garden. Paying for gardening work can be expensive and many local "gardeners" prefer to concentrate on straightforward jobs like lawn mowing rather than time-consuming tasks such as digging and weeding.

Looking at Existing Gardens

Once you have thought out your ideas about the sort of garden you want, you might wish to draw up a checklist of everything you need. You might also have a look at some existing garden designs for ideas and inspiration. Apart from the sample gardens on the Geoff Hamilton 3D Garden Designer, you might have a look at some real rather than "virtual" gardens. A visit to Barnsdale in Rutland to see the actual gardens used in Geoff Hamilton's television programmes should provide all the motivation you need.

Drawing Up a Rough Site Plan

Before starting to design your garden on the computer, you need to go outside and draw up a rough site plan, outlining the boundaries of your plot. The rough plan will also show the positions of major features which are to remain, such as fences, paths and manhole covers. You will need to resort to the traditional pencil and paper and you will also need a tape measure, string and pegs and preferably an assistant to help with the measuring. A compass should be used to determine the orientation of your garden in relation to North, enabling you to sketch the areas in the sun and shade at different times of the day, also affected by the presence of any large trees or buildings. This may dictate the location of any seating areas and sites for sun-loving plants and perhaps a vegetable plot.

The computer design will be based on X, Y co-ordinates, which you may remember from your school days. The X and Y axes are horizontal and vertical lines, in this example graduated in metres, as shown below. The X and Y axes cross at a point known as the *origin*, also described as the position (0,0) since it's at the beginning of both scales.

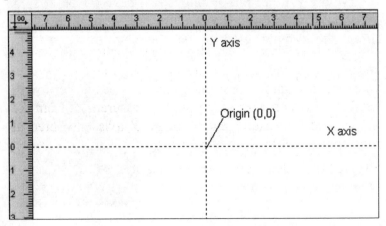

As shown in the previous screenshot from the 3D Garden Designer, the screen is mapped out with rulers graduated in metres. We can place the origin, i.e. position (0,0), anywhere we like on the computer screen. We can also place features and objects in their correct positions, provided we know their distances in metres from the X and Y axes. We therefore need to set up some X and Y axes outside on the actual garden, using pegs and string, and then measure the distances to the fences, boundaries, paths, etc. These can then be transferred to the computer screen to give an accurate representation of the real garden.

First you must decide how the garden is to be displayed on the computer screen. You might decide to line up a house wall or fence with the left or right side of the screen. Or you might decide to find North using a compass in the garden, then place this at the top of the screen in the centre.

Now, using a long piece of string and pegs, place a straight line from the top of your garden (the part which will appear at the top of the computer screen) to the bottom of the garden. This corresponds to the Y axis shown on the previous page. Now construct another straight line using pegs and string, at right angles to the first. This corresponds to the X axis in the diagram on the previous page.

You can now measure the distances in metres from the X and Y axes to all of the main boundaries and features in your existing garden. For each object or feature you will need to record on your rough plan a measurement from the X axis and a measurement from the Y axis, measured at right angles to the pieces of string.

In mathematical shorthand, an object placed 5 metres from the Y axis and 4 metres from the X axis would have a position (5,4), as shown by the small fishpond below.

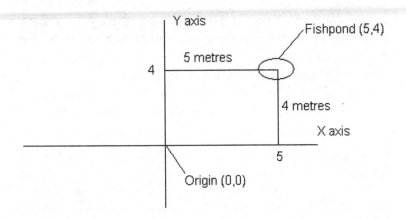

This will enable the feature to be accurately located when the plan is transferred to the computer, as discussed shortly.

Testing Your Soil

The type of soil in your garden (acid or alkaline) can be identified using one of the pH testing kits available from garden centres, etc. Together with details of any damp or very dry areas, this will influence your choice of plants, trees and shrubs. Reference to one of the plant encyclopedias described in this book should ensure that any plants you select will flourish and thrive in the conditions prevailing in your own garden.

Next

Once your rough plan is drawn and your soil is analysed, you are ready to start using the computer. The next chapter describes the installation and basic features of Geoff Hamilton's 3D Garden Designer software.

Getting Started on the Computer

Introduction

This chapter assumes you are new to computing; jargon is avoided as far as possible, but in case of difficulty you may find Appendix 2 helpful. Most of the garden design work in this book will involve the use of a mouse.

Mouse Operations

Click

This means a single press of the left mouse button. The cursor is placed over an object on the screen, such as a *menu option* or an *icon*. A click will cause, for example, a command to be carried out or a further menu to appear. When you click over an object in a garden design in **Plan** view, the object is *selected or highlighted* in red.

Double-click

This means pressing the left mouse button very quickly, *twice in succession* and is often used to start a program from an icon on the Desktop, the main opening screen in Microsoft Windows.

Right-click

This involves pressing the right button while the pointer is over a screen object. A "context-sensitive" menu appears with options relating to the selected screen object.

Dragging and Dropping

This entails clicking over an object on the screen, then, while keeping the left button held down, moving the mouse pointer, together with the object, to the new position. Release the left button to place the object in its new position. This method is used to move plants and garden objects into new positions in the 3D Garden Designer.

Installing the Software

This requires copying certain files (or information) from the 3D Garden Designer CD onto your computer. This is a one-off operation and once completed needn't be repeated.

First insert the 3D Garden Designer CD into your CD drive. After a few seconds the GSP logo appears and then a copy of the **LICENSE AGREEMENT** is displayed.

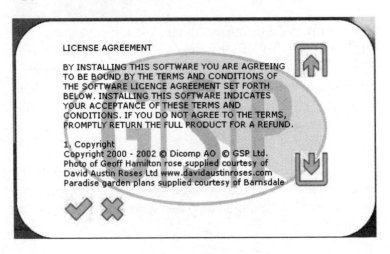

In order to continue with the installation you must click the tick showing that you agree to be bound by the terms and conditions of the agreement.

After clicking the tick, the following window appears, displaying various pictures and icons representing the different parts of the 3D Garden Designer software package.

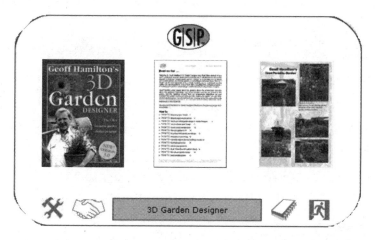

The parts of the package are described later but for the time being, click the picture of the cover of Geoff Hamilton's 3D Garden Designer package, as shown below.

This starts the **Setup** program which will install the software on your computer's hard disc drive. Don't worry about the technicalities of this - you can complete the installation by simply clicking the **Next** button on all of the various "windows" or boxes which appear on the screen. These boxes or windows, known as *dialogue boxes*, display information and request responses from you.

On clicking the **Next** button you are told the location where the 3D Garden Designer program will be saved on your hard disc.

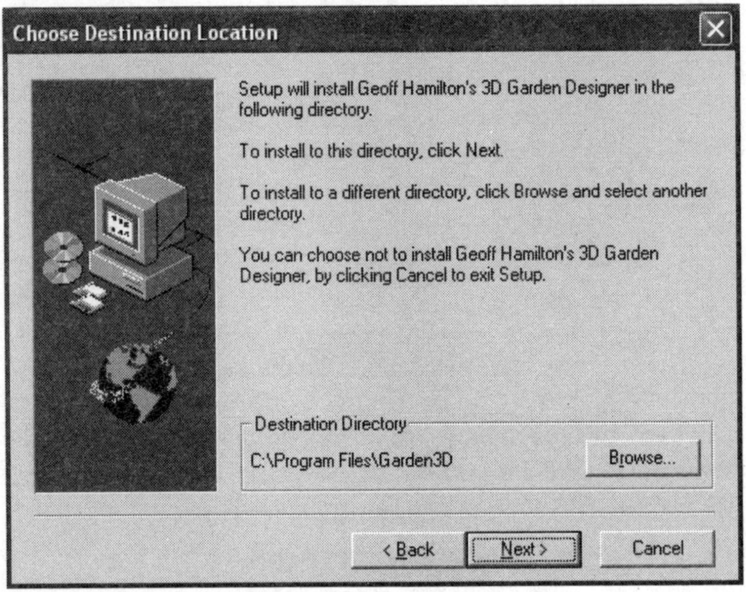

Click **Next** to accept the suggested location as shown above under **Destination Directory**.

You are now given a choice of how much of the software is to be installed - some parts of the package are optional.

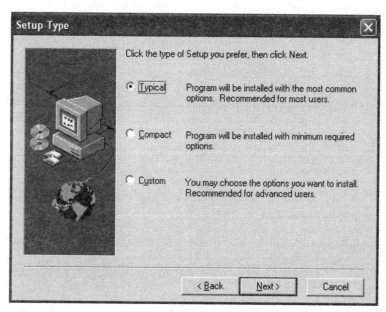

Most users are recommended to use the **Typical** setup option as shown selected above. However, if your computer is short of hard disc space, you may wish to select the **Compact** setup. This will only install the most essential components of the software. The **Compact** installation is selected by clicking in the small circle (known as a *radio button*), as shown above and below.

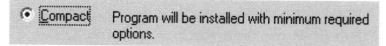

The **Custom** setup, shown in the dialogue box above, is for more advanced users who wish to make their own selections of the parts of the software to be installed.

Click **Next** again to create icons for the **3D Garden Designer** software then finally click **Next** and **Finish** to complete the installation process.

The installation process will have placed an icon for the **3D Garden Designer** (shown on the right) on the **Windows Desktop**. The Desktop is the main Windows screen which appears after the computer starts up, showing the icons for your commonly used programs.

If you double-click the icon on the Windows Desktop as shown above, the Geoff Hamilton 3D Garden Designer is launched ready for you to start work.

Another way to launch the program is to use the menus in Windows XP. Click *start*, **All Programs, 3D Garden Designer**, and **Geoff Hamilton's 3D Garden Designer**, as shown below.

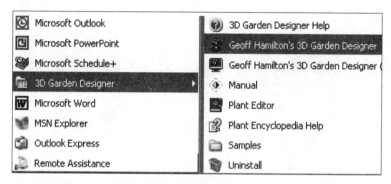

Running the Program

Having completed the installation, you can now run the 3D Garden Designer program whenever you want to. The program can be started by the two methods just described, i.e. by double-clicking the icon on the Windows Desktop or from the *start*, **All Programs** menus.

The CD must be present at all times!

You must make sure the CD remains in the drive whenever you try to run the program. If the CD is not present, the error message shown below will appear. **D:** is the label for the CD drive on most computers.

You can also start the program by placing the CD in the drive. After a few seconds the following window is displayed.

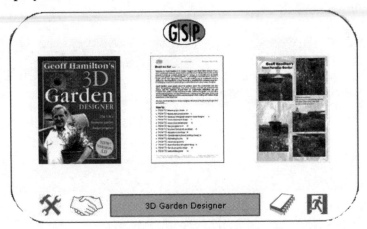

As described earlier, you can start the program by clicking on the 3D Garden Designer picture on the left above. All of the other pictures and icons are links to features and services. Clicking the GSP logo shown above and right connects you to the GSP website.

The picture of a page of text above is a link to a manual which can be printed out on paper. Clicking the page of photographs on the right above displays Geoff Hamilton's Paradise Gardens, as part of a document which can be viewed on the screen or printed on paper.

The two icons shown on the left above are website links for Technical Support and Product Registration.

The two icons on the right above are firstly a link to a technical support guide followed by the icon for exiting the program.

On starting the program, the initial screen will usually be blank. You can have a look at a sample garden plan by selecting **File** and **Open...** from the Menu Bar across the top of the screen.

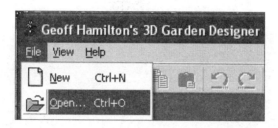

The sample gardens are on the **D:** drive in the **SAMPLES** folder, as shown below. Now click on one of the gardens on the list shown below. This highlights the file.

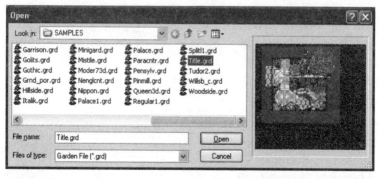

In the above example, the selected garden was given the name **Title** when it was originally saved. This is called the *file name*, used to identify the file when it is saved on the computer's hard disc. After the file name is the extension **.grd** as in **Title.grd**, and **Gothic.grd** above. The extension **.grd** is a label denoting the type of file, in this case a garden design. You may have seen other file name extensions such as **.doc** for a word processing document.

On clicking the **Open** button as shown on the previous page, the sample garden **Title.grd** is displayed, as shown below.

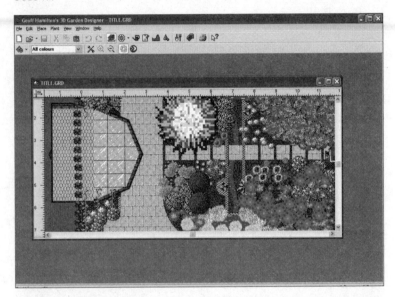

As can be seen above, the garden does not occupy the whole of the computer screen. This is controlled by the three buttons shown on the top right of the above window, known as Minimise, Maximise and Close, reading from the left.

The Maximise Button

Click this to make the window fill the entire screen.

The Minimise Button

Click this to reduce the window to an icon on the Windows Taskbar at the bottom of the screen as shown below on the right.

The Restore Button

After a window has been maximised, the Maximise Button changes to the Restore Button shown right. Clicking this reduces the window to its original size.

Closing a Window

To shut down the current window, click the Close Button, marked with a cross, in the top right-hand corner of the screen.

After clicking on the Maximise icon shown on the right, the sample garden **Title.grd** completely filled the screen, as shown below.

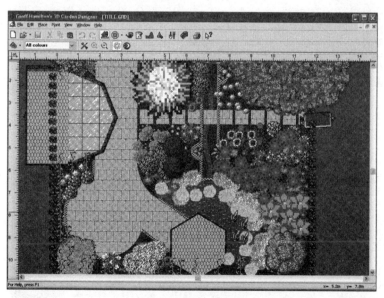

Notice the horizontal and vertical scales along the top and left-hand side of the screen and the origin 0,0 near the top left-hand corner. As discussed shortly, we can move the origin to any position we like on the screen.

Experimenting with the Sample Garden

Shortly we will discuss creating your own garden design on the computer. However, here are a few exercises to help you get the feel of the program.

In this example, the sample garden **Title.grd** has been opened from the 3D Garden Designer CD. Move the mouse cursor about the screen and notice how the position of the cursor is displayed in metres on the bottom right of the screen, above the time. These are the x and y measurements discussed in Chapter 2.

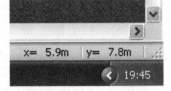

Now move the mouse over the hexagonal green building at the bottom of the screen. This is an arbour, one of the many structures provided in the 3D Garden Designer.

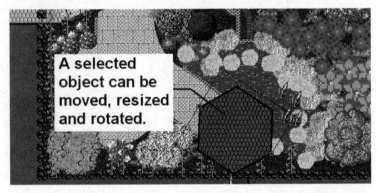

A selected object can be moved, resized and rotated.

With the cursor over the arbour, click the left mouse button. The arbour changes from green to red. It is now highlighted or *selected* and is ready to be *moved, resized* and even *rotated*.

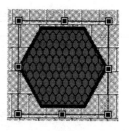

The selected object is surrounded by a square frame with eight small black squares around its perimeter. Experiment by dragging these squares to enlarge or reduce the size of the arbour. Now place the cursor inside of the arbour and *keeping the left-hand mouse button held down,* move the arbour to a new position on the screen by moving the cursor about an inch or 2 or 3 cms. This is called *dragging.* Release the mouse button to place the arbour in its new position. Note how the x and y measurements at the bottom of the screen have changed to reflect the new position of the arbour.

Note also how the cartoon man used as the cursor changes to illustrate different operations, such as moving an object or waiting on a bench while the computer is working.

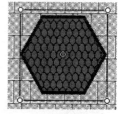

If, after clicking to select a screen object such as the arbour, you again click inside the object, the eight black squares are replaced by four white circles, as shown on the right. There is an additional circle containing a cross in the centre of the arbour. If you drag one of the outer white circles, the arbour is rotated about the centre circle. You can move the centre circle by dragging to a new position, to give a new centre of rotation.

If you click over a tree in one of the sample gardens, you will find a more limited range of operations possible. A tree can only be dragged to a new position. If you select a bed of flowers, the bed can be enlarged by dragging. This increases the number of flowers in the bed.

The curved path shown below was extracted from the **CASTLE.GRD** sample garden plan loaded from the 3D Garden Designer CD.

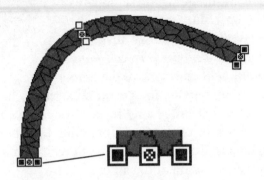

After selecting the path by clicking, various "handles" or small boxes appear, as shown above. You can alter the curve of the path by dragging the boxes containing the crossed circles. Dragging the black boxes alters the width of the path; for example, making the path wider or narrower, as shown below.

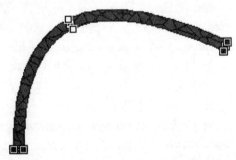

If you click the path again while it is already selected, white circles appear, allowing you to rotate the path about a moveable centre, displayed as a crossed circle as before.

Experiment with other objects and see if they can be resized, rotated, or whatever. Don't worry about "damaging" the designs - any changes will only be temporary. When you close the garden you will be asked if you want to save the changes, to which you can answer **No**.

Now double-click on any one of the plants in the sample garden. (*Double-clicking* means giving two clicks of the left-hand mouse button in quick succession). A window similar to the one shown below should appear, giving full planting details of the selected flower, shrub or tree.

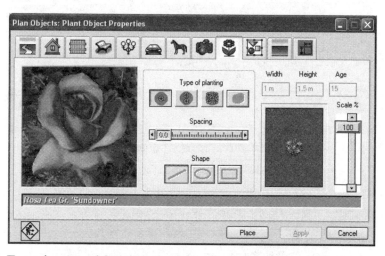

Experiment with other features in the sample garden, e.g. flowers, plants, shrubs, paved surface areas, buildings and other garden structures and furniture. Try changing some of the details in the **Object Properties** window which appears, as shown above, when you double-click over an object.

Viewing in 3D

Select **Window** and **3DView** from the menu bar across the top of the screen. Try "walking" through the garden by dragging with the mouse or using the cursor (arrow) keys.

Select **Window** and **Plan** to return to the main **Plan** view, in which the designing and editing of a garden takes place.

Closing the Sample Garden

To leave the sample garden without saving any of the changes caused by our experimentation, click **File** and **Close** from the Menu Bar. The following window appears.

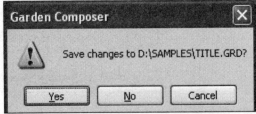

In this case click **No** so that none of the editing changes are saved. The program then returns to a blank screen ready for you to start work on another garden

4

Exploring the 3D Garden Designer

Introduction

This chapter describes in more detail the various features in the 3D Garden Designer. At the end of the chapter you should be ready to create a garden design on the computer.

The 3D Garden Designer is "driven" by a series of *menus* and *icons*. If you're not familiar with these terms, a typical menu is shown below. This is a *drop-down* menu, which appears when the word **Plant** on the Menu Bar is clicked.

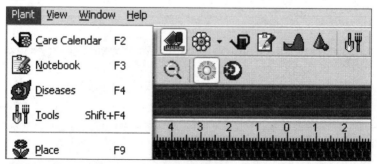

The small pictures are known as *icons* and usually represent an operation. For example, clicking the icon shown on the right opens up the built-in plant encyclopedia, discussed later.

In the screen shot below, the sample garden **CHATEAU.GRD** has been loaded from the CD, as described in Chapter 3.

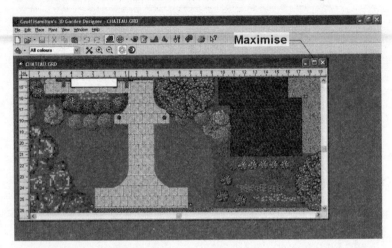

Note that the above garden is shown in a small window; as previously described the window can be made to fill the screen by clicking on the Maximise button in the top right of the window.

At the top of the main window above is the Title Bar, also shown enlarged below.

The Title Bar displays the name of the program and the name of the garden design which is currently open, **CHATEAU.GRD** in this example. (The name of the garden is assigned by the user when the garden is first saved).

On the right-hand side of the Title Bar are the 3 buttons for Minimising, Maximising and Closing the window.

The Menus

Beneath the Title Bar is the Menu Bar, shown below, starting with the words **File, Edit, Place**, etc.

A single click on any of the words opens a drop-down menu, such as the **File** menu shown below.

If you don't like using a mouse, keyboard alternatives are given at the side of each menu option, as shown above. For example, to start a new garden design, instead of clicking the blank page icon or the word **New** as shown above, you could use **Ctrl+N**. This means "keep the **Ctrl** key held down and press the **N** key."

An overview of the main functions of the various menus now follows.

The **File** menu shown on the previous page is common to most computer programs and is used for operations like opening a new or existing garden and for saving and printing gardens you have created.

The **Edit** menu shown below allows you, amongst other things, to *cut* or *copy* selected sections of a garden design and "paste" them elsewhere - perhaps into another garden altogether. You can also *insert* pictures into a design.

The **Place** menu allows you to insert all sorts of structures, buildings, animals and garden objects into your design.

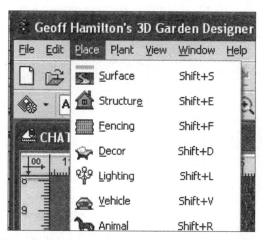

Each of the menu options above leads to a further menu giving a choice of objects to place in the garden.

For example, selecting **Structure** presents a list of buildings and other garden objects which can be placed in the garden, such as the **Custom tower** shown below.

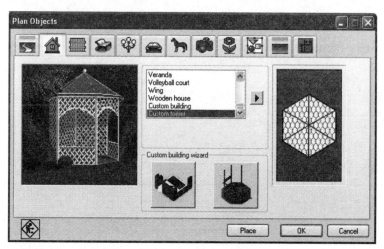

The **Plant** menu provides a wealth of information about the plants in a particular garden design.

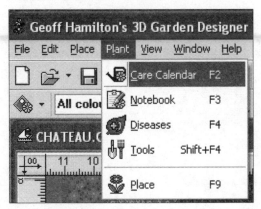

First click over the plant or group of plants (or trees) in the garden. This selects or highlights the plant(s). Then click the **Care Calendar** option on the **Plant** menu. A calendar is displayed showing the operations needed to look after the plant (or tree) throughout the year.

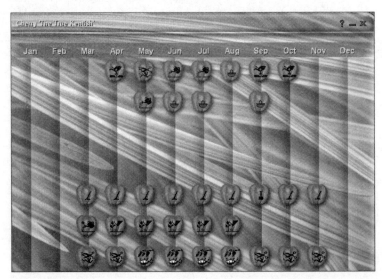

Similarly, by clicking **Diseases** on the **Plant** menu shown on the previous page, a list of common diseases for the selected plant or tree appears.

The **Notebook** option on the **Plant** menu allows you to type in your own notes about the plants currently selected in the garden design. The **Tools** option gives details of over 300 different garden tools.

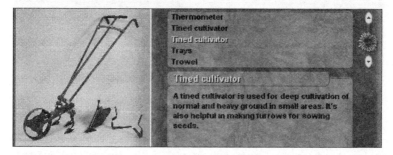

The **Place** option on the **Plant** menu allows you to select plants from the plant encyclopedia and plant them into your new garden design, arranged in various ways.

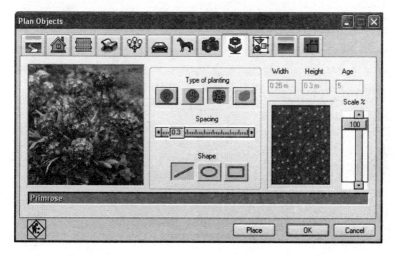

The **View** menu shown below allows you to switch various screen features on and off.

If there is a tick next to an item, the item is displayed on the screen. If you don't want an item displayed, click in the box to remove the tick. **Main Toolbar** shown above refers to the row of icons under the Menu Bar, shown below and also in the above screen extract.

————**Main Toolbar**

The **Plan Toolbar** option listed in the above **View** menu refers to the shorter row of icons shown below and also partly visible in the above screen extract.

————**Plan Toolbar**

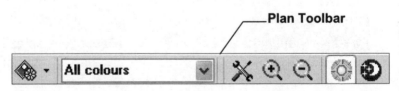

The meanings of the icons in the **Main Toolbar** and the **Plan Toolbar** above are given shortly.

Referring to the **View** menu on the previous page, the tick against the word **Rulers** switches on the horizontal and vertical scales shown on  the right. The rulers are also visible on the screen extract near the top of the previous page.

The **Status Bar** listed in the **View** menu is a rectangular strip across the bottom of the 3D Garden Designer window. As you move the cursor about the screen, the **Status Bar** displays helpful information. When the cursor is over a particular **Toolbar** icon, the **Status Bar** explains the function of the icon. For example, when the cursor is over the icon shown on the right, the **Status Bar** displays the following: ___**Status Bar**

```
Activate '3D Plan' window of current document
```

As you move the cursor about within a garden plan, the **Status Bar**, (shown below in a shortened form) displays the position of the cursor as measurements relative to the x and y scales, discussed in Chapters 2 and 3.   ___**Status Bar**

```
For Help, press F1          x= 4.9m   y= 16.6m
```

Obtaining On-screen Help At Any Time

As shown on the **Status Bar** on the left above, you can call up **Help** information on the screen by pressing **F1**, one of the specially programmed *function keys* along the top of the keyboard.

The **Plan...** option on the **View** menu, allows you to control several aspects of the way a garden is viewed.

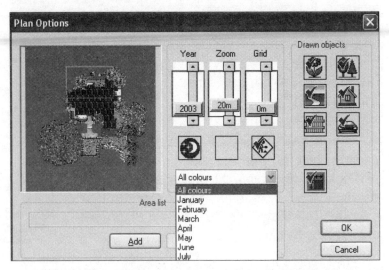

The **Year** slider allows you to see how the garden should look in a few years time. The **Zoom** slider enables you to take close-up or distant views of parts of the garden.

If you want to display horizontal and vertical guidelines, these can be set at various distances using the **Grid** slider. Setting the **Grid** slider to zero means no grid is shown. Items ticked under **Drawn objects** above, are displayed on the garden design.

The icons on the right allow you to switch between day time and night time views of the garden. The drop-   down menu shown above under **All colours** allows you to see the colours of the garden after selecting various months of the year. The **All colours** option shows all plants in their best colours.

The **Window** menu controls the display of the on-screen boxes or windows.

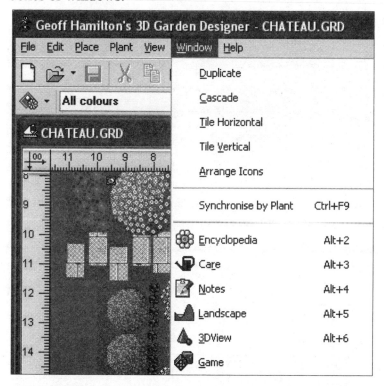

Duplicate as shown in the above menu allows you to make a copy on the screen of a window and all of its contents.

You can have more than one window open on the screen at the same time, displaying more than one garden.

Cascade, Tile Horizontal and **Tile Vertical** refer to different ways of displaying multiple windows. **Cascade** arranges the windows behind one another, like a pack of cards, but with the title of each garden visible, as shown on the next page.

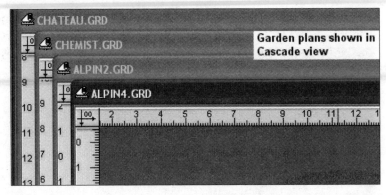

Tile Horizontal displays two open windows one above the other. Tile Vertical displays the windows side by side. With four windows open on the screen, horizontal and vertical tiling both produce the same result, as shown below.

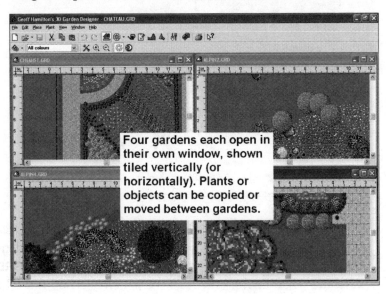

Referring back to the Window menu on page 45, **Arrange Icons** is used to make sure all of the icons are clearly visible at the bottom of the screen, and not obscured by other windows. These icons represent windows which have been *minimized*.

For convenience the lower part of the **Window** menu is shown again below.

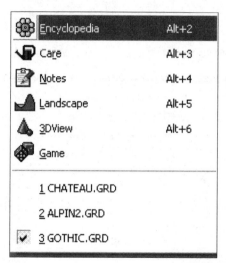

The three entries at the bottom, **CHATEAU.GRD**, **ALPIN2.GRD** and **GOTHIC.GRD** represent three gardens currently open on the screen. The tick against **GOTHIC.GRD** indicates that this is the *currently active* window. The active window is the one open for editing and working in. To make another window the active window, simply click anywhere within the window.

The Plant Encyclopedia

The **Encyclopedia** option on the Window menu on the previous page opens up the built-in plant encyclopedia containing comprehensive details of 3700 plants.

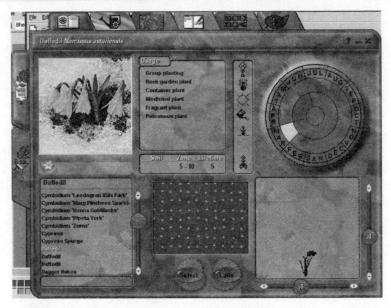

There is also a standalone program, Geoff Hamilton's Plant Encyclopedia, available as a separate package. Plant Encyclopedias are discussed in more detail later.

Plant Care

The **Care** option on the previous Window menu displays a list of maintenance tasks for all of the plants in the currently selected garden. Tasks for different months can be viewed by scrolling the **Care** window, as shown on the next page.

Plant total		Name	◄	October			November
123	🏵	Blue Alpine Daisy		🔅			
17	🌿	Boston Ivy		🌱 🌿	/		⚘
14	🏵	Camass		🗃			
2	🌲	Canadian Hemlock		🌱	/	🗡	/
2	🌳	Cherry 'The True Kentish'		🌱	/	🗡	/
5	🌲	Cheshunt Pine		🌱	/	🗡	/

In the above **Care** window, the different tasks are represented by icons, as shown on the right. Click on a particular icon to find out what task it represents.

For example, clicking on the shears icon brings up the following information about light pruning.

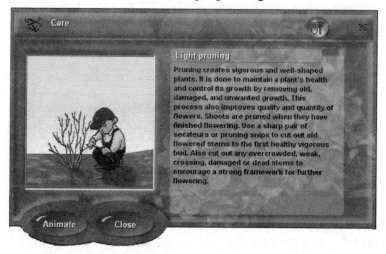

The **Animate** button above presents a moving cartoon demonstrating how to perform a particular task such as pruning.

Adding Your Own Notes

Continuing down the **Window** menu, the next option is the **Notes** feature, as shown in the menu extract on the right. This allows you to type in your own notes about the current garden. These notes are saved along with the garden design.

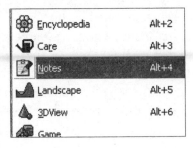

Landscape View

The **Landscape** option above is used if you have a sloping garden or one containing mounds or hillocks. The basic garden is shown in black and white, but contour lines representing areas of different heights can be shown in different colours. These areas can be infilled in colour.

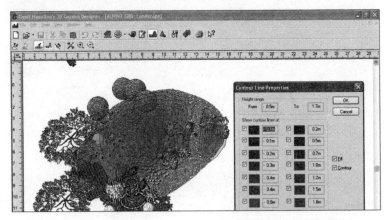

To return to the **Plan** view, click the **Plan** option which now appears on the **Window** menu, replacing the **Landscape** option shown earlier.

Viewing in 3D

As mentioned earlier in this book, a garden can be viewed in 3 dimensions. Simply click **3DView** from the **Window** menu. You can use the cursor keys to scroll through the garden. Any number of cameras can be placed at different positions in the garden, enabling you to check your design from different angles. Colours of flowers and foliage can be shown as they will appear at different times of the year.

Once the 3D view is displayed, the **Window** menu changes to display a **Plan** option instead of the **3DView** option shown earlier. This enables you to return to the **Plan** view to continue editing and designing.

Plan	Alt+1
Encyclopedia	Alt+2
Care	Alt+3
Notes	Alt+4
Landscape	Alt+5
Game	

It is possible to have both the **3DView** and the **Plan** view open at the same time in separate windows. This is done by opening the garden in plan view then selecting **3DView** from the **Window** menu. Then select **Window** and **Tile Vertical** to see both windows side by side on the screen, as shown below.

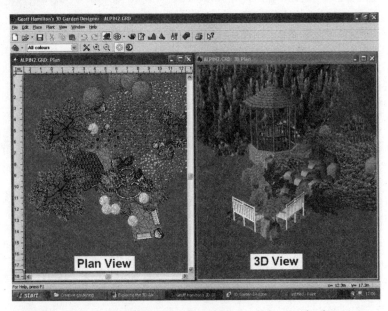

Changes can be made in the **Plan** view and these are reflected in the **3DView**, although there might be a short delay while the **3DView** is updated.

The final option on the **Window** menu is a game to test your plant knowledge. You must either name a plant from its picture or select the correct picture given the name of the plant.

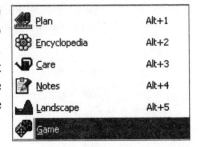

Obtaining Help

The **Help** menu shown right allows you to contact the software company GSP on the Internet by selecting **GSP on the Web**. **Context Help** allows you to find help on objects and menus around the screen. Click on **Context Help**

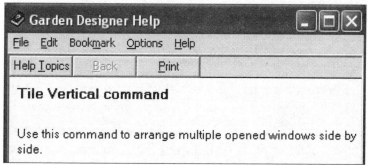

and the cursor changes to the arrow head and question mark shown left and in the menu above. Now click over the screen object or menu option you need help on. For example if you click over the **Tile Vertical** option on the **Window** menu, the following help information appears.

Similarly if you click over an object in the garden plan, the following description might appear.

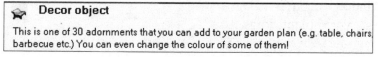

Help can also be obtained by highlighting the required screen object or menu option then pressing the **F1** key.

Context-sensitive Menus

Another set of menus, which don't appear on the Menu Bar
in the 3D Garden Designer, can be displayed. These are
known as *context-sensitive menus*; they "pop up" whenever
you *right-click* over an object on the garden design in **Plan**
view. The menus are different depending on the object
selected. For example, if you right-click over a *paved area*
the following **Surface Object** menu appears.

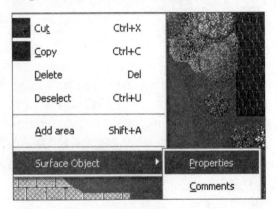

The **Properties** option shown above allows you to check the
details of the paved area and make changes, if necessary.

If you right-click over a *plant* in the garden design the **Plant
Object** menu appears, this time giving options relevant to
the choice and care of plants.

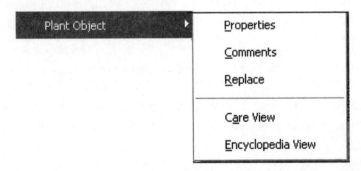

The Toolbars

Beneath the Title Bar on the 3D Garden Designer screen are the **Main Toolbar** and the **Plan Toolbar**.

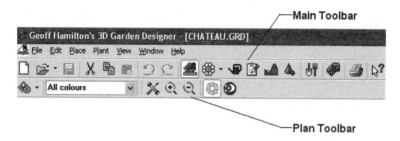

The icons on the toolbars are *shortcuts* to various operations. Many of the operations can also be launched from the menus discussed earlier in this chapter. The advantage of the toolbar icons is that the operation is launched by a single click of the mouse. As mentioned earlier, in order for the toolbars to be displayed on the screen, a tick must appear against their names in the **View** menu shown on the right.

A brief note on the function of each icon can be seen by allowing the cursor to hover over the required icon, as shown below for the **3D Plan**.

The Main Toolbar

The function of each icon on the **Main Toolbar** is now explained, working from left to right along the Toolbar.

 Start a new garden design on a blank sheet.

 Open an existing garden design which has been saved on the hard disc or on a CD.

 Save the current garden design on your hard disc or on a recordable CD, (discussed later).

 Cut (i.e. remove) a selected object or area of the garden. The selection is placed in a temporary store called the *clipboard*.

 Copy a selected object or area of the garden. The selection is held on the clipboard.

 Paste an object or area of a garden from the clipboard onto another part of a garden or onto another garden, e.g. with two gardens open side-by-side in their own windows.

 Undo and **Redo** a previous operation. A quick way to correct a mistake.

Select the **Plan** view, the main view for designing your garden and making changes. Use this icon to return to the **Plan** view from the **3DView** or **Landscape** view.

 Open up the built-in plant encyclopedia, giving full details of plants and common diseases.

 Launch the **Care Calendar**, giving monthly maintenance tasks for all of the plants in the current garden.

 Open the **Notes** window, allowing you to type in and save your own notes about any aspect of the garden.

 Display the garden in **Landscape** view, with contour lines showing any small hillocks, etc.

 Display the garden in **3DView** using cameras placed in different positions by the user.

 Open the **Tools** window, describing gardening tools suitable for the currently selected plants.

 Open up the botanical game, allowing you to test your knowledge of plant names and pictures.

Set up the printer and produce a "hard copy" of your garden design on paper.

 Obtain **Context Help** by clicking objects on the screen. Can be used on menu options, icons and objects in a garden plan.

The Plan Toolbar

If the **Plan Toolbar** is not visible, select **View** and make sure there is a tick against **Plan Toolbar**.

 Place a new object in the garden design, such as a **Surface**, **Structure**, **Fencing**, etc.

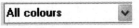 This displays all of the plants in their best colours, regardless of the month. Click the down arrow to view the plant colours in different months.

 Set options for viewing the garden plan, such as day or night, zoom in or out and grid lines.

 Zoom in and out of the current garden design.

 Switch between day-time and night-time views of the garden.

5

Designing the Hard Landscaping

Introduction

At this stage, if you have followed the previous chapters, you will have started to get the feel of the 3D Garden Designer and many of its features. In this chapter we start work on the computer, carrying out the "groundwork" for a new garden, by putting in place the hard landscaping - the fencing, walls, paved areas and paths, etc. This is followed by the addition of structures such as an arbour or summer-house and features like a pond and a waterfall. The next two chapters deal with the selection and planting of flowers, trees and shrubs.

To make an accurate design on the computer, you will need a sketch plan as discussed in Chapter 2. This should have all of the important measurements including the boundaries and distances to the main features, measured from the x and y axes, as described in Chapter 2.

Start up the 3D Garden Designer by inserting the CD in the drive and clicking the Geoff Hamilton picture. Alternatively you can either double-click the icon on the Windows Desktop or select *start*, **All Programs**, **3D Garden Designer**, 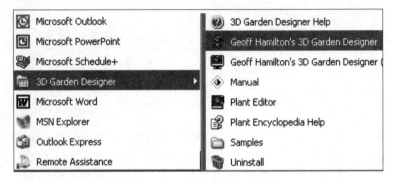 and **Geoff Hamilton's 3D Garden Designer**, as shown below.

Microsoft Outlook	3D Garden Designer Help
Microsoft PowerPoint	Geoff Hamilton's 3D Garden Designer
Microsoft Schedule+	Geoff Hamilton's 3D Garden Designer (
3D Garden Designer ▶	Manual
Microsoft Word	Plant Editor
MSN Explorer	Plant Encyclopedia Help
Outlook Express	Samples
Remote Assistance	Uninstall

You will probably be presented with a screen showing one of the existing gardens. Click **File** and **New** to start a brand new garden or alternatively click the **New** icon on the **Main** **Toolbar**. The screen should clear to give a green background. This will be used as a lawn, forming the background to our garden design. All other features will be placed over the top of the lawn.

You may also need to maximize the window for the garden design, to make it fill the whole screen, using the button shown on the right and discussed in detail earlier.

Saving a Garden Design

At this stage it's worth saving your garden design - even though it's still only like a blank canvas. Once you have saved a garden design with its own name, further saving is much simpler, only requiring a single click of the left mouse button. Now click **File** and **Save As...** from the menu bar. The **Save As** dialogue box opens as shown below.

Delete the default title **UNTITLED1.grd** shown above, and enter a name of your own. This can be anything you like but should be relevant to your garden so that it can easily be identified in future.

You don't need to enter the **.grd** extension to the file name - this is done automatically. Now click the **Save** button shown above to save a copy of the (blank) garden design on your computer's hard disc (usually the **C:** drive).

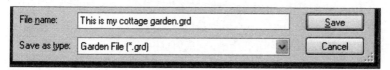

Creating a New Folder

Notice in the **Save As** dialogue box on the previous page, there is a folder called **Garden Designs** listed in the **Save in:** bar. This is a folder I have created especially for this work. You can create a folder of your own after clicking on the **Create New Folder** icon shown right and on the previous page. Give the folder a meaningful name, replacing the words **New Folder** shown on the right. Then you can use this folder for all of your garden designs in the future.

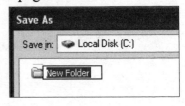

Alternatively you could save all your garden designs in the **My Documents** folder in Microsoft Windows. This is provided for saving all of the files you create.

Important!

It is vitally important that you are able to save your garden designs reliably and regularly. It's also essential that in future you can locate your garden designs in their folder on the hard disc. Otherwise hours of work may be wasted.

Once your garden design is set up with a file name such as **This is my cottage garden.grd** in a folder such as **Garden Designs,** all future saving can be carried out by a single click on the save icon on the **Main Toolbar** and shown on the right.

Further Reading

Please note that important topics such as saving your work and creating new folders are covered in more detail in my book "Computing for the Older Generation" also from Bernard Babani (Publishing) Ltd (BP601).

Setting Up the Screen

When you open a blank garden design ready to start work, the x and y axes or scales are shown across the top and down the left-hand side of the screen, respectively.

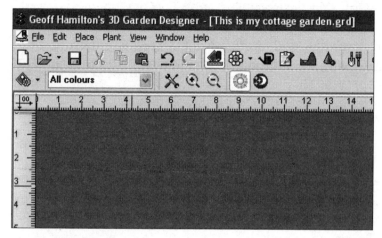

Setting the Zoom

The 3D Garden Designer can be used for gardens of all shapes and sizes. You need to set the zoom, so that your garden is easily visible, neither too small nor too close up. You can alter the zoom using the two buttons on the **Plan Toolbar** shown right and above. Another method for very large gardens is to place a small object, such as a chair, in the top left-hand corner of the garden. (From the menus, use **Place**, **Decor**, select an object then click **OK**. The object, such as a chair, can be moved by dragging). Next, using the measurements on the x and y rulers, scroll down to the bottom right of the garden and place another garden object. Now zoom out and the program will automatically adjust the zoom to show your garden in full.

Setting the Origin

The x and y scales shown on the previous page have the origin or starting point 0,0 in the top left-hand corner of the screen. To use this arrangement you will need to know your actual measurements from a corresponding point on the top left of the sketch plan.

If, however, you have used (on your sketch plan) x and y axes which cross roughly in the middle of the garden, as shown on the next page and described in Chapter 2, you need to move the axes or scales on the computer. Fortunately this is quite simple.

To move the origin or point 0,0 to a point in the middle of the screen, place the cursor over the intersection of the two scales in the top left-hand corner of the screen. Now drag the 0,0 icon shown as (**00**) on the right, to the required position on the screen. (To restore the origin 0,0 to the top left-hand corner double-click in the top left-hand corner as shown).

You can display the x and y axes as lines on the screen by clicking over the appropriate x or y ruler. Then drag the cursor across or down the screen. A horizontal or vertical line appears, which can be dragged and dropped into position as either the x or y axis. The two lines should be adjusted to cross at the position 0,0. These lines will not appear when the garden is printed. To remove the x or y axis, simply drag the line and drop it over the appropriate ruler.

The rulers will help to set the boundaries of your garden. Objects can be moved around by dragging and positioned precisely using the rulers, according to your sketch plan.

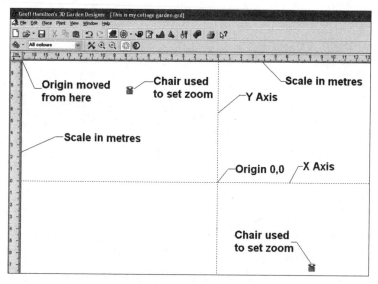

Displaying Grid Lines on the Screen

The screen can be mapped out in a grid of vertical and horizontal lines. This makes it easier to place a garden object accurately on the plan. Some garden objects such as a summer-house, for example, can be resized by dragging the corner "handles". The grid lines help to estimate the finished size. The spacing between grid lines can be set at 1, 2, 5, 10, 20 or 50 metres apart. As shown below, garden objects such as furniture or water features can be made to "snap to the grid lines", discussed on the next page.

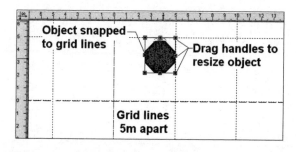

The grid lines are set using the **Plan Options** dialogue box, launched by clicking on the icon (shown on the right) on the **Plan Toolbar**.

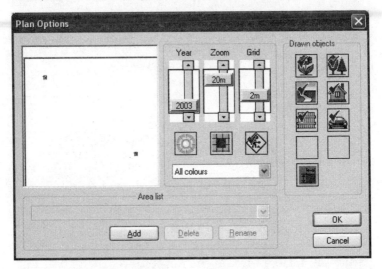

The grid spacing is set by dragging the **Grid** slider shown above. When the slider is set at zero, no grid is shown.

The icon in the middle shown above and right is the **Snap to Grid** feature. To switch on the **Snap to Grid** feature, click on the icon. A red tick should appear in the icon. After you move

an object on the screen, **Snap to Grid** automatically moves the object hard up against the nearest grid line. This is useful, for example, to place several objects in a straight line.

Also shown above is the **Zoom** slider, giving another way of adjusting the view on the garden, either close-up or at a distance.

A Simple Garden Design

The following is a simple plan which incorporates many of the tasks involved in creating a garden design on a computer. Each task is explained shortly.

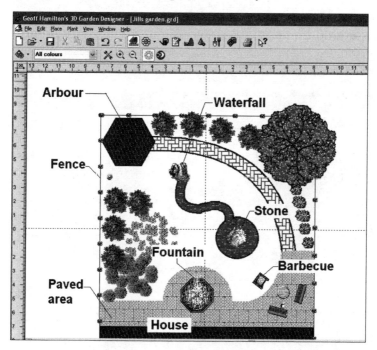

For clarity in the above screenshot, the background was set to white. Similarly, although 1m grid lines were used in drawing the garden, they have been switched off for the above illustration. Please refer back to the above diagram, while working through the remainder of this chapter.

Reminder - Save Regularly

Click the **Save** icon, shown on the right, every few minutes to make sure your hard work isn't lost if there's a power cut or computer problem.

Working with Boundaries

The background colour of the entire garden can be set by selecting **Place, Background** and then choosing your background from the grid of colours, before clicking **OK**.

The boundaries are usually defined by fences or walls. In this example a house is to form the lower boundary of this particular garden. Select **Place, Structure** and then choose **Brick House** from the dialogue box shown below.

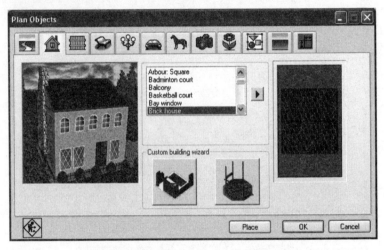

When you click **OK** the house is placed on your plan view. It can be moved into position on the grid lines by placing the cursor inside and dragging. The house can be resized by dragging on any of the black squares around its perimeter. The grid lines below are set at 1m spacing.

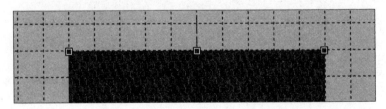

Placing a Fence or Wall

Select **Place** and **Fencing** to open the **Plan Objects** window
shown below. A large choice of fences and a brick wall
are available by scrolling down the menu shown in the
centre below. (Walls are handled in a similar way to
fences in the 3D Garden Designer).

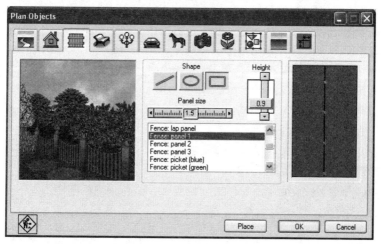

You can alter the panel size and the height of the fence
using the sliders shown above. If you need to *curve* the
fence, select the line icon for
the **Shape** as shown on the
right and above. Click **OK** to
place the fence onto the garden

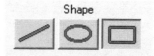

plan. If you need several pieces of fencing, click on **Place**
once for each piece of fencing, before clicking **OK**.

Several operations are needed to adjust the angle of the
fence, the length, position and any curvature, as described
on the next page.

Manipulating a Fence or Wall

A length of fencing including posts is shown below.

Click once on the fencing and some small squares containing black circles appear as shown below.

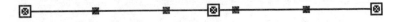

Changing the Length of a Fence

The fence can be lengthened or shortened by dragging on the small squares containing black circles, shown above.

Moving a Fence

To move the fence, click anywhere between the squares shown above and drag the fence to another position, before releasing the left-hand mouse button.

Applying Curvature to a Fence

Click to display the small squares (each containing a cross in a black circle) as shown below. Drag any of the squares to obtain the shape of curve required.

Please note that quite wide surfaces for paths, etc., can be curved in a similar way, provided the **Shape** is set using the line icon as shown on the right and on the previous page.

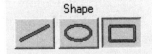

Rotating a Fence or Wall

A fence may need to be rotated to the angle required in the garden. With the **Shape** of the fence set as a line, as discussed previously, click once to display the squares containing black circles. Now click again and, as shown below, a black circle and some white circles appear.

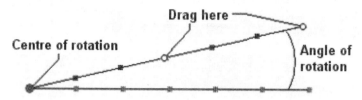

Drag any of the white circles and the fence rotates. The black circle acts as the centre of rotation. The black circle can be moved by dragging to give a new centre of rotation.

Changing an Existing Fence

If you want to alter the properties of a fence, etc., double-click anywhere on the fence to bring up the **Plan Objects: Fencing Object Properties** window shown below.

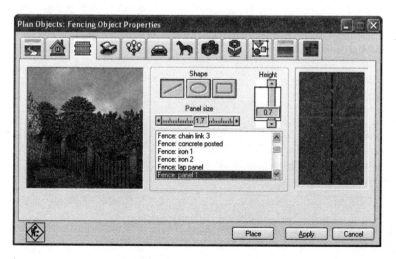

Placing a Path and Border

First we will look at the long curved path and border
leading to the **Arbour**, as shown on page 67. Select **Place**
and **Surface** and choose the type of surface you require, as
shown below.

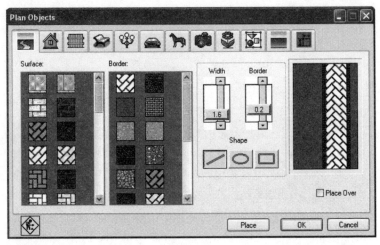

Please note that the scrollable list under **Surface:** shown
above includes water as well as the various types of
paving, etc. Notice that you can set the width of the path
using the **Width** slider shown above. As the path is edged
with a border select the border material from the samples
shown under **Border:** above. The width of the border is set
by adjusting the **Border** slider.

Please note that a surface will normally appear as the top
layer, above grass, etc. However, if one surface overlaps
another, the last surface to be added may be obscured by
the original surface. To show a surface above other
surfaces, click the check box next to **Place Over** in the
above screenshot, so that a tick appears.

Manipulating a Path or Surface

As the path is going to be curved, we must select the line icon under **Shape** in the previous screenshot.

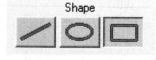

Click **OK** to place the path or paved surface, etc., onto the garden design. Click anywhere in the path to select it. The path should now appear red, with several handles as shown below.

Altering the Width

The width of the path or surface can be altered by dragging any of the black squares shown above. The width of the border is adjusted by dragging the white squares.

Altering the Curvature and Length

The squares containing the crossed black circles are used to alter (by dragging) both the curvature and the length of the path or surface.

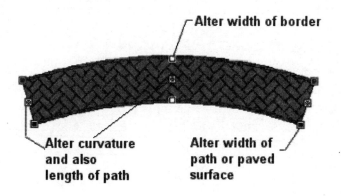

┌Alter width of border

Alter curvature and also length of path

Alter width of path or paved surface

Rotating a Path or Surface

The path or surface can be rotated after clicking anywhere on the surface, then clicking again, but not in rapid succession. Some white circles and a black circle appear.

As described earlier in the section on fences, a path or surface can be rotated by dragging one of the white circles. The black circle acts as the centre of rotation. If necessary, the black circle can be moved to a new position by dragging.

Moving a Path or Surface

The path can be moved by clicking anywhere within it and dragging to its new position. Click anywhere outside of the path to remove the selection, i.e. restore the finished colours of the path or surface and remove the handles. As shown below, grid lines set at 1m spacing make it easy to place the path accurately in its final position.

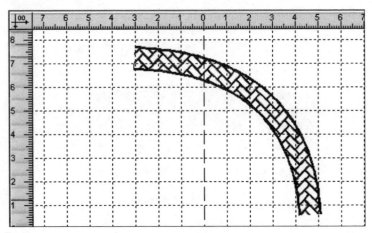

Creating a More Complex Paved Area

The paved area shown on page 67 is more complex than
the shapes we have covered so far. However, it is made up
using exactly the same methods discussed earlier.

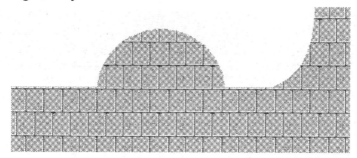

First the material for the paved area is selected from **Place**
and **Surface**. Then the paved
area can be made up from the
three shapes selected in the **Plan
Objects** window under **Shape**:

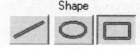

Shape

1. A circular area, drawn after selecting the
   icon shown on the right.

2. A curved area, as described previously,
   drawn after selecting the line icon shown
   right.

3. A series of rectangles to fill in the remainder of the curved surface, drawn after selecting this icon.

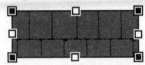

When several paved sections are joined together, the lines between pavings are adjusted so that they appear correctly.

Grouping Several Shapes Together

The paved area on the previous page was made up of several different shaped areas - a circle, a curve and two rectangles, as shown below. It can be useful to *group* these shapes together into a single entity. This is done by holding down the **Shift** key while each shape is clicked in turn. Then right-click over the composite area as shown below and click **Group** from the menu which pops up.

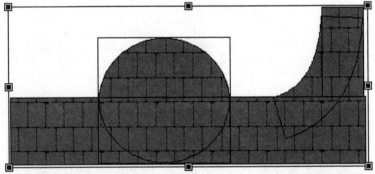

Now the group of shapes can be moved and resized as if it were a single object. To rotate the group about a centre as a single object, click the selected group again and drag one of the white circles which appear.

Creating the Water Feature

The water feature on page 67 consists of a waterfall, a small stream or rill, followed by a circular pond with a large stone in the centre.

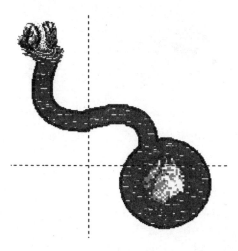

First the waterfall was selected from **Place** and **Décor** and scrolling down to **Water: waterfall 1**, as shown below.

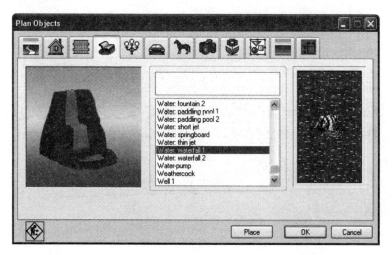

Manipulating the Waterfall

After clicking **OK**, the waterfall is placed on the plan.

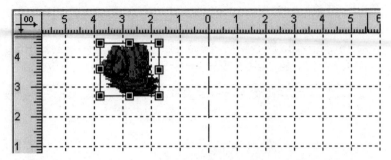

The waterfall can be enlarged or made smaller by clicking to select it and then dragging on any of the black squares shown above. The waterfall can be moved to its exact position by dragging, using the horizontal and vertical rulers as a guide. To make this easier the grid lines have been switched on using the **Plan Options** window selected by the icon on the **Plan Toolbar**, shown right. The grid spacing has been set at 1m. This is described in detail on page 66.

The waterfall can be rotated after clicking twice, but not in rapid succession. White circles appear which can be dragged to rotate the waterfall about a centre. The centre of rotation is shown as a black circle. This can be moved by dragging.

Placing Garden Objects in General

The above methods for placing, moving, resizing and rotating the waterfall also apply to most objects in the 3D Garden Designer. Some objects, such as vehicles, furniture and animals are available in a standard size. They can be moved and rotated but cannot be resized.

Creating the Stream and Pond

The small stream or rill was created in exactly the same way as the path discussed earlier. After selecting **Place** and **Surface**, the list of surface materials as shown below was scrolled to the bottom, where the blue surface representing water was selected. A narrow border was also applied.

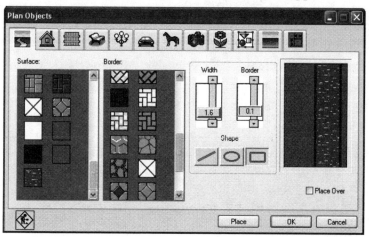

In order to curve the stream the **Shape** must be set as a line as shown right and above under **Shape**. The stream was made as two separate curved pieces in the same way as the path described earlier.

These can then be moved into their final position by dragging and rotating as described earlier.

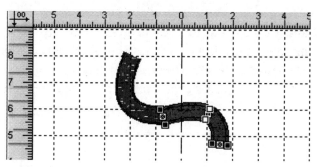

The pond was created in exactly the same way as the stream except that a circular **Shape** was

 selected from the **Plan Objects** window shown on the previous page.

This can be resized and dragged like the other objects in the garden.

The stone in the centre of the pond was selected after clicking **Place** and **Décor** and scrolling down the **Plan Objects** list. Moving and placing the stone was as previously described for the other garden objects.

The hexagonal arbour shown on page 67 was selected from the **Plan Objects** window after clicking **Place** and **Structure**.

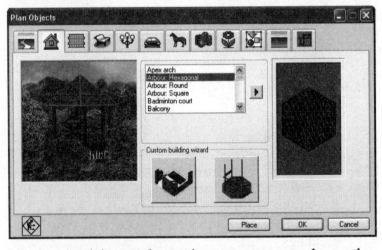

Moving, resizing and rotating structures such as the arbour, fountain and barbecue are as described for other garden objects described earlier in this chapter.

Garden furniture such as the table and chairs can be selected from **Place, Décor** and **Plan Objects**, but resizing is not possible with these standard objects.

Other Hard Landscaping Features

There are many other garden objects, including various buildings, tennis courts, lighting, animals and vehicles. However, the methods of placing and manipulating them are similar to those already discussed in this chapter.

The **Plan Objects** window gives access to the **Custom building wizard**, which allows you to design and modify buildings using your own dimensions and materials.

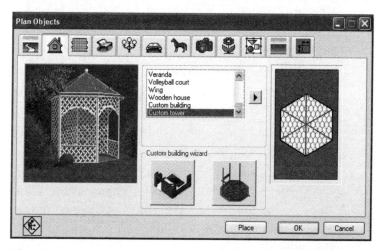

The first part of the **Custom building wizard** is the **House wizard** accessed by the left-hand icon shown above and on the right. The **House wizard** helps you to create and modify houses and other buildings such as sheds and greenhouses.

The **Tower wizard** accessed by the right-hand icon shown above and on the right helps you to create and modify arbours, arches, chimneys and conservatories.

Summary: Working with Garden Objects

The general methods for placing and manipulating garden objects, such as paths, paved areas, structures, fences and water features can be summarized as follows:

- An object is chosen from the **Plan Objects** window, accessed from the **Place** menu. The object is placed on the garden design after clicking **OK**.

- To *select* an object, click within the object. A selected object is highlighted in red and usually displays "grab handles" or squares around its perimeter. Click outside of an object to *deselect* it.

- To *move* an object around the screen, place the cursor over the object and "drag" to its new position. Then release the left-hand mouse button.

- To *resize* an object, select the object then drag one of the squares to make the object bigger or smaller.

- To create a *curved* object such as a fence, wall or path, select the line icon as the **Shape** in the **Plan Objects** window. When the object is selected in the garden plan, drag the crossed black circles to create the required curve.

- After selection, click an object a second time to reveal white circles and a black circle. Drag the white circle to *rotate* the object about the black circle, which is a movable centre of rotation.

- Several objects can be joined together to form a *group*. This can then be resized, moved and rotated *as a single object*. To form a group, click each object in turn while holding down the **Shift** key. Then right-click and select **Group** from the menu.

6

Selecting Plants

Introduction

This chapter describes how the computer can be used to help with the selection of plants prior to placing them on your new garden design. The 3D Garden Designer includes a built-in encyclopedia covering nearly 4000 plants, with comprehensive descriptions and details of their care and maintenance.

Obviously the choice of the plants in a garden depends very much on individual preferences, but a few general points to consider might be as follows:

- In a small garden, beware of trees which may grow unacceptably high. For example, disputes between neighbours over fast-growing leylandii hedges can escalate into legal battles with serious consequences. Roots which damage paths and buildings may also lead to conflict.

- Shrubs, trees and climbers can be used as *screening* to obscure unsightly objects such as buildings, fences, or motorways, etc.

- Garden maintenance can be reduced by using ground cover plants to cut down on weeding.

- Careful choice of plants, evergreen trees and shrubs can ensure colour and interest in the garden throughout the winter months.

- The relative heights of plants, shrubs and trees will affect the view from different parts of the house and garden. The **3DView** in the 3D Garden Designer will allow you to check these views. The garden plan can then be modified, if necessary. This might arise if, say, a shrub was likely to grow and obscure a much-loved view from the house of a perennial border or bird-feeding area.

- Planting in your garden will be affected greatly by local conditions:

  For example, the soil may be acid or alkaline and either wet or well-drained. This will determine what sort of plants will thrive in your garden.

  Depending on your location, the climate may be relatively cold and wet or warm and dry. Your garden may enjoy sunshine all day or parts of it may have long periods in the shade.

  Plants may need to be hardy or require extra protection from strong prevailing winds. Protection might take the form of shrubs, trees, or fencing.

The following pages show how the built-in plant encyclopedia can be searched to find plants which match your personal requirements and local conditions as outlined above. Then the plants can be placed on the garden design in **Plan** view before being moved to their final position.

The 3D Garden Designer Plant Encyclopedia

With a choice of nearly 4000 plants, the built-in plant encyclopedia in the 3D Garden Designer should allow free rein to your creative ideas. (In addition to the built-in plant encyclopedia in the 3D Garden Designer, there is also the Geoff Hamilton Plant Encyclopedia available separately on its own CD and described in Chapter 10).

If you can't find the exact plant you require, the 3D Garden Designer will allow you to make a close substitution - near enough for you to evaluate your garden design in both **Plan** view and **3DView** and to print a working plan. This will be helpful in any discussions with suppliers, contractors, etc.

The plant encyclopedia can be started with a single click on the flower icon on the **Main Toolbar**, shown on the right. If you click the small down-arrow to the right of the flower, a drop-down menu appears as shown below and discussed later.

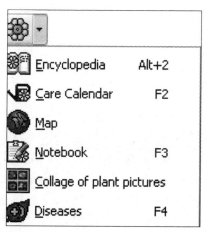

The plant encyclopedia can also be launched by clicking **Window** and **Encyclopedia** from the Menu Bar.

The main plant encyclopedia opens up as shown below.

During this work you will probably wish to alternate your screen display between the plant encyclopedia and the main **Plan** view. This can be done by cycling through the current programs in your computer using **Alt** and **Tab**. (This means while holding down the **Alt** key, keep pressing the **Tab** key).

Alternatively you can look at the Taskbar at the bottom of the screen, where the current programs are shown.

Clicking one of the names on the Taskbar above will either:

- Open the program on the screen in its own window.

- Minimise or "shrink" the program to just an icon on the Taskbar.

Displaying Plant Information

There are two main modes of operation for the
plant encyclopedia, selected by tabs on the left-
hand side of the encyclopedia window. The upper
tab selects the main information display for the
encyclopedia, as shown on the previous page.
With the upper tab selected, a window appears
showing initially all 3701 of the plants in the encyclopedia.
You can scroll down the list (by dragging the leaf on the
slider shown on the right below) looking at different plants
until you find what you want.

Or if you know the name of a particular plant you can type
in the first few letters into the bar at the top of the list. In
the above example you would first delete **Iris 'Classic
Look'**. If for example, you typed in **Lily**, the encyclopedia
would immediately jump to the relevant part of the plant
list showing all of the lilies in the encyclopedia.

Referring to the screenshot on page 86, a button in the lower centre of the window allows you to switch between **Latin** or **Common** plant names.

Referring to the top half of the plant encyclopedia shown below, the name of the selected plant appears across the top left-hand corner over the main window.

On some plants there are a few small icons under the main photograph. Clicking on these small icons brings up additional
photographs of the plant. If an apple tree is selected, for example, a cutaway photograph of the fruit is shown.

In the middle of the screenshot above, the **Usage** panel lists typical planting arrangements and uses for the selected plant.

The vertical strip on the upper right of the plant encyclopedia displays a number of icons giving details of the selected plant's characteristics and preferences. The meaning of each of these icons is displayed if you allow the cursor to hover over the icon. For example, for the Lily 'Antarctica', working from top to bottom, the icons indicate that this is a bulb, likes a moderate temperate, full sun and occasional watering. The bottom three icons show that the Lily 'Antarctica' is easy to care for, fast growing but slow to spread.

On the top right of the plant encyclopedia, several rings are shown with the months of the year around the outside.

The ring immediately inside of the months shows the colour of any flowers, fruit, berries or blossom throughout the year. The inner ring shows the colour of the foliage throughout the year.

In the centre of the plant encyclopedia is a small panel indicating preferred conditions for the selected

plant. The first two icons represent well-drained and heavy soils. (Allow the cursor to hover over the icon to reveal the soil type.) Other types of soil include acid and alkaline.

The **Zone** figure shown above is an indication of the plant's ability to withstand low temperatures. Low zone numbers represent cold minimum temperatures. In the United Kingdom the Zones range from 7 in Scotland to 9 in the South West. If you want to grow a plant requiring a higher zone number than the number in your location, then greenhouse protection will be needed in winter.

The **Lifetime** figure above is an approximation of the number of years the plant will live, but this might be extended with good plant care.

In the lower middle of the plant encyclopedia is a picture of how the selected plant might look when planted in a group. This is shown on the left below. The side view on the right below has two sliders indicating the height and spread of the plant.

More About Tabs

The display of basic plant information just discussed was obtained after selecting the upper tab on the left-hand side of the plant encyclopedia, as shown below. In order to display this basic plant information we must also select the first tab across the top of the plant encyclopedia, shown below and on the right.

The information displayed applies to the plant currently selected in the lower left-hand panel of the plant encyclopedia.

The Upper and Lower Tabs

The upper tab on the left-hand side of the window, which displays information, must remain selected for the work which follows on the next few pages. The lower tab will be used shortly when we *search* for plants meeting certain criteria, known as *filtering*. The next section looks at the other tabs along the top of the plant encyclopedia window, starting with the second tab, the Plant Care Tab.

The Plant Care Tab

This tab shows maintenance operations on a
month-by-month basis for the selected plant.

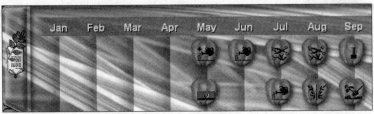

The meaning of each icon shown above can be revealed by
clicking on the icon.

Advisory notes about the selected care task are given in the
right-hand panel. Some **Care** windows display an **Animate**
button, as shown above. Clicking the **Animate** button plays
a moving visual demonstration of the process in the left-
hand panel.

The remaining tabs across the top of the plant encyclopedia
are now discussed

Countries of Origin

The third tab from the left across the top of
the plant encyclopedia produces a window
showing (in green) the part of the world
where the selected plant originates from. A slider enables
you to zoom in and out of the map. Right-click an area on
the map to display a description of the climate of the
region, as shown below.

Map Usage

Brasilia, Venezuela, Bolivia, Paraguay

In this zone the climate varies from humid tropical to humid subtropical. In
different parts of the zone the average winter temperature fluctuates from 23
to 29oC, and the relative air humidity is very high. In countries with a
moderate climate plants from this zone can be grown only indoors or in
greenhouses. The plants should be kept at a constant temperature (20-22oC,
without sharp temperature drops in the wintertime). Many plants from this
zone (e.g. orchids) require a short (1-2 month) dry period in the winter.
Watering should be reduced but the plants not allowed to dry out.
CAUTION: It is best to use soft water with a low calcium and magnesium salt
concentration for watering most plants from this zone

The Notes Tab

You may wish to add your own notes about a particular
plant, perhaps about possible suppliers and prices, etc. The
Plant Notebook is opened after clicking the fourth icon
across the top of the plant encyclopedia, as
shown on the right. A blank page appears with a
flashing cursor, ready for you to start typing. The
notes are saved together with the garden design.

The Picture Collage

This icon presents a grid of thumbnail (i.e. miniature) pictures of all of the plants in the plant encyclopedia or in a reduced list produced by the **Filter** (discussed later).

The currently selected plant is outlined in a yellow frame. Clicking on another plant makes it the selected plant. Its details will then be displayed if you switch back to another tab, such as the basic information tab on the top left. If you double-click on the thumbnail for a plant, an enlarged photograph is displayed. Buttons at the top right allow you to switch between thumbnail images and a  slideshow and to move forward and backwards, one at a time, through the selected images. You can also use the scrollbar and **Page Up/Page Down** and cursor keys to move through the thumbnails.

Pests and Diseases

The rightmost tab across the top of the plant encyclopedia provides information about problems which can afflict plants. With a plant selected in the left-hand panel of the plant encyclopedia in the basic display mode, i.e. with the upper left-hand tab and the left-hand tab across the top selected, click the Pests and Diseases icon shown on the right above. The following window appears.

The Pests and Diseases window above operates in two ways. If **All** is selected using the button at the bottom right of the window, diseases affecting all of the plants in the encyclopedia are displayed. In effect this option displays a comprehensive encyclopedia of known pests and diseases.

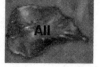

If the **Current** button is selected at the bottom right of the window shown on the previous page, then only those diseases which affect the selected plant are shown.

The **Filter** button shown on the previous Pests and Diseases window allows you to find out which plants are affected by a particular pest or disease. Select the pest or disease in the bottom left-hand panel. When you click the **Filter** button you are returned to the basic display window. This now displays a reduced list of plants, i.e. only those susceptible to the plant or disease.

In the Pests and Diseases window shown on the previous page, pictures or photographs appear in the top left-hand panel. Additional pictures may be viewed after clicking the small icons which may appear underneath the main picture.

Text describing the damage done by pests and diseases and methods of control is displayed in the **Symptoms** and **Control** panels shown on the previous page.

Searching for Plants Using the Plant Filter

The lower left-hand tab, as shown on the right, launches the Plant Filter which allows you to search for plants meeting various requirements such as colour, height, preferences, etc. The Plant Filter responds with a list of plants meeting your criteria.

The Plant Filter uses the same set of tabs across the top of the plant encyclopedia window as shown earlier in the section on displaying plant information. However, instead of selecting plants from their names, as before, we now select plants according to criteria entered under each of the tabs. This is described for each tab, working across the screen from left to right.

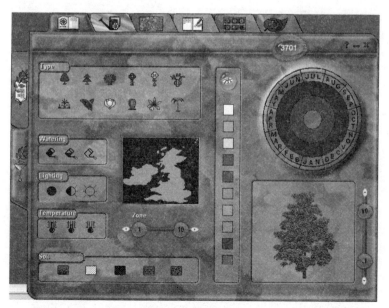

Please note that the number on the top
right of the plant encyclopedia window
indicates the total number of plants in
the current selection. Initially this is set

at 3701, the total number of plants in the
encyclopedia. However, as we add more
criteria, e.g. by specifying red flowers,
the list is reduced as the unwanted plants
are filtered out. To restore the full list of

plants (back to 3701), click on the reduced number.

Searching Using the Basic Plant Information Filter

With the Filter tab selected on the left side
and the first tab selected across the top, we
can search for several different basic plant
criteria. The top left-hand panel, shown

below, allows you to select the plant **Type**. Allow the
cursor to hover over an icon to display its meaning.

Reading from left to right along the top row above, the
plant types are: **Deciduous trees, Coniferous Trees, Bushes,
Flowers, Bulbs and Climbers**.

The icons on the second row above represent **Herbs
Grasses, Ferns, Vegetable/Fruit, Cacti/Succulents, Orchids
and Palms**.

Underneath the **Type** panel is a small frame showing the **Watering** criteria. You can look for plants that need **Constant**

Watering, Occasional Watering or **Water only when Dry**.

The **Lighting** criteria allow you to search for plants that prefer **Full Shade, Half Shade** or **Full Sun**.

Similarly the **Temperature** criteria enable you to choose **Warmth-Loving Plants**, those liking a **Moderate Temperature** or **Frost-Resistant Plants**.

When searching for plants that will thrive in your own garden you need to know the soil type. This can be determined using one of the soil testing kits available from garden centres. Your own soil type can be entered in the **Soil** criteria in the plant encyclopedia filter shown below.

The various soil types reading from left to right above are: **Well-drained, Alkaline, Acid, Heavy** and **Poor Soil**.

Please note that you may not always see the full list of icons displayed for a particular criterion. For example, if you have already selected a plant **TYPE** which does not like alkaline soil, then that icon will not appear in the **Soil** panel as shown above.

As you enter criteria, you may see the map of the United Kingdom change in the centre of the window. Areas where

your chosen plants will grow successfully outdoors are shown in green. If, for example, you have selected **Orchids** as the plant **Type**, successful outdoor growth is mainly limited to western areas of Britain and coastal areas of Ireland. If you live outside of the areas marked green then you will need to grow the plants under cover. The slider below **Zone** above shows that orchids need to be grown in Zones 9 and 10.

The vertical column in the centre of the window shown on page 97 and in part on the right here allows you to specify the colours of your required plants. By clicking the icon shown at the top, you can alternate the list between flowers, fruit, leaves and autumn leaves. The wheel on the right of the plant encyclopedia (on page 97) shows the months when these colours of flowers, leaves, etc., will be displayed.

The slider at the bottom right of the window (on page 97) allows you to specify the maximum and minimum heights of the plants you want to find, as shown here on the right.

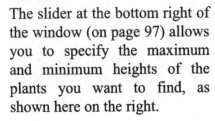

Searching Using the Plant Care Filter

To search for plants meeting certain plant care criteria we need the Filter tab selected on the left-hand side and the Plant Care tab (shown on the right) selected from across the top.

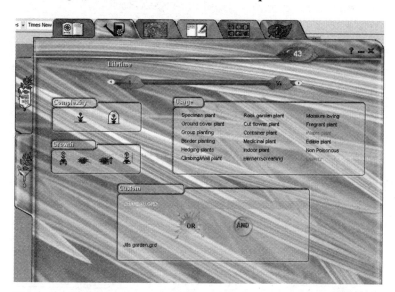

The sliders near the top of the plant encyclopedia, shown below, allow you to specify the life of the plant, within a range initially set from 1 to 99 years.

The **Complexity** icons shown on the right give a choice between plants which are easy to care for and those which are difficult.

You can search for plants according to their rate of growth, as shown on the right. Reading from left to

right, the growth icons represent: **Slow spreading**, **Quick spreading**, **Slow growing** and **Fast growing**.

The **Usage** panel below allows you to specify the purpose or application of your required plants.

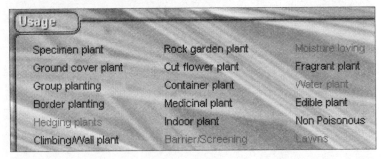

In this example, the plant **TYPE** had previously been selected as **Cacti/Succulents** in the basic plant information Filter, as discussed earlier. Plants of this particular type are not suitable for certain uses, such as **Hedging plants**, and so these uses are greyed out on the **Usage** panel shown above. You can obtain a detailed description of a usage by double-clicking on the usage listing in the panel shown above.

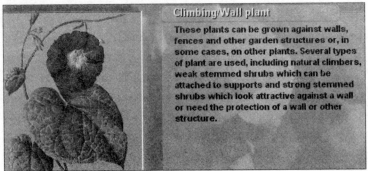

Climbing/Wall plant

These plants can be grown against walls, fences and other garden structures or, in some cases, on other plants. Several types of plant are used, including natural climbers, weak stemmed shrubs which can be attached to supports and strong stemmed shrubs which look attractive against a wall or need the protection of a wall or other structure.

The **Custom** panel shown below allows you to limit your uses to those plants in an earlier garden design.

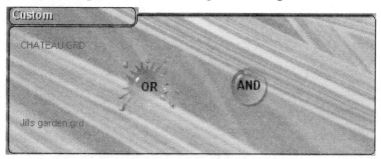

The first garden can be opened by double-clicking on the upper line of text shown above, in this example, as **CHATEAU.GRD**. This launches the **Open** dialogue box allowing you to find and select the chosen garden.

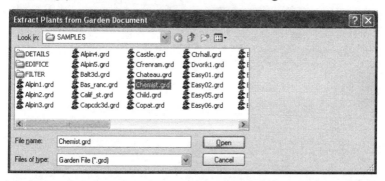

You can also select a second garden after double-clicking the lower line of text above, **Jills garden.grd**.

The **OR** button above allows you to limit the uses of plants in your new garden design to those uses found in *either* of the two selected garden designs. The **AND** button above allows you to limit the uses of plants in your garden to those uses found in *both* of the selected garden designs. The **OR** and **AND** buttons appear 'splashed' when selected.

Searching Using the Plant Location Selector

Clicking on the Filter tab and the tab shown right displays a map of the world. Click on an area to find plants from that region. For an extreme example, select **Sahara, Arabian peninsular.** Only two plants are found, as shown below. These can be displayed by clicking the left upper tab and the leftmost tab across the top, to display basic plant information.

Using the Note Finder Filter

If you've previously entered your own notes for various plants, you can find plants containing certain words in the notes. The following dialogue box appears when you select the Filter tab and the Notes tab across the top, shown right.

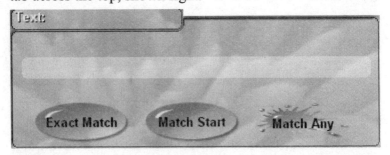

When entering keywords in the bar shown above, you must use upper or lower case letters to match the original notes. You can enter the whole word or just a few letters. Click the **Apply** button to find and display the plants containing the keywords in their notes.

Using the Picture Collage Filter

With the Filter tab on the left-hand side of the plant encyclopedia selected, click the **Picture Collage** tab as shown on the right.
Photographs of all sorts of different plants are shown.

If you select one of the photographs a yellow frame appears around the selection and the number at the top right of the window changes from 3701 (the total plants in the encyclopedia). For example, when you select the picture of a cabbage, the number displayed changes to 21, the number of cabbage-type plants in the encyclopedia. If you now click the upper left-hand tab (shown on the right), the
Picture Collage widow displays only the pictures of the 21 selected plants.

Clicking the Plant Information tab (shown on the right) with the upper tab selected on the left-hand side, displays detailed information of the plants in the cabbage selection, including the extract from the plant list shown below.

Using the Pests and Diseases Filter

With the Filter tab selected, click the rightmost tab (Pests and Diseases) shown on the right. A grid of thumbnail pictures appears allowing you to select either a type of plant or a common pest such as a cat. If you now click the upper left-hand information tab, symptoms of known damage and diseases are displayed. The example below involves damage to pine needles.

> **Symptoms**
>
> Pineapple-like forms, several cm in diameter, appear on branches.

Methods of control are also displayed, as shown below.

> **Control**
>
> The plants are sprayed with insecticides in April or in September when the aphid is not protected with galls. If the damage is insignificant, this treatment is not necessary.

Adding Plants to the Garden Design

Introduction

The last chapter showed how you could use the plant encyclopedia built into the 3D Garden Designer in two basic ways:

- If you know a plant's name, you can find it in the list in the plant encyclopedia and display a description of the plant and how to care for it.

- You can search the library of 3701 plants and find those plants meeting certain criteria such as height, colour, months of flowering and preferred growing conditions like the soil type and sunshine/shade.

When suitable plants have been identified in the plant encyclopedia they can be placed on the garden design, after specifying the planting arrangements such as spacing and configuration, e.g. planting in straight lines, circles or rectangles. Once the plants are placed on the garden design they can be manipulated, bent into curves, etc., and dragged into their final position - although you can always alter the planting configuration and move the plants if you're not happy. A major advantage of design on a computer is that changes can be made ad infinitum.

7   Adding Plants to the Garden Design

The result of the hard landscaping work described in Chapter 5 is shown below. This is the starting point for the planting work which follows. For clarity in this illustration the background has been set to white, rather than the usual lawn (or whatever). The lawn or other type of background can easily be reinstated after clicking **Place** and **Background**.

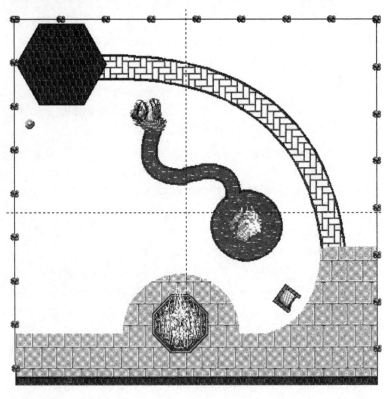

Planting a Tree

Suppose you wanted a tree in the top right-hand corner of the garden shown on the previous page. If you don't know the name of a suitable tree, you could enter your search criteria in the Plant Filter as described in the last chapter. For example, you might enter the height of a deciduous tree, type of soil, amount of sunshine preferred, etc.

The computer responds with a shortlist from which, for example, you might choose a **Rowan**, as shown below.

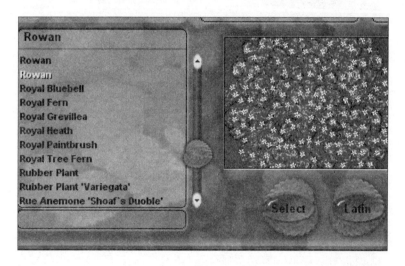

Now click the **Select** button at the bottom of the window, as shown on the right and above. This opens up the **Plan Objects** window shown on the next page, where you select the planting configuration such as the spacing between plants. You can also set the age of the plant and therefore the initial height and width at the time of planting.

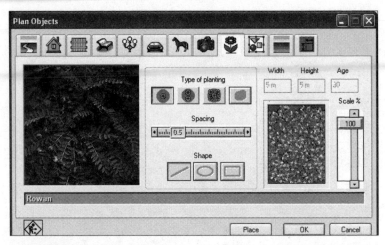

As shown above, you can set the **Type of planting**, either singly, in a line or in groups. You can also adjust the distance between plants by dragging the slider shown above under **Spacing**. As you change the spacing, the small plan view (shown above under **Width** and **Height**) is changed accordingly.

As discussed earlier in the chapter on hard landscaping, there are three shapes which allow planting in virtually any layout. The line icon under **Shape** above and on the right enables plants to be arranged in a straight line or in a curve. The other two icons under **Shape** allow plants to be arranged in an oval or a circle and in a rectangle or a square.

On the right of the above window you can see the **Width** and **Height** of the plant after a certain number of years' growth, determined by dragging the slider, which has a range of between 0% and 100% of the plant's lifespan, as shown on the next page.

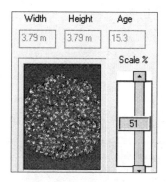 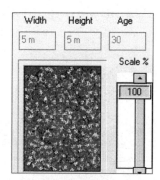

When you click **OK** the tree is placed on the plan as shown below. The Rowan tree appears on the plan on the screen selected in red with a frame round the outside. However, there are no squares or "grab" handles to allow you to resize or rotate the tree. (The tree's size is determined by the **Scale** slider shown above).You can, however, move the tree by clicking anywhere inside the tree and dragging it into its correct position.

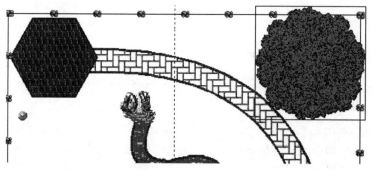

Reminder - Save Regularly

Click the **Save** icon, shown on the right, every few minutes to make sure your hard work isn't lost if there's a power cut or computer problem.

Manipulating a Line of Plants

Next we will plant a line of shrubs in a curve, shown below between the Rowan tree and the arbour (the hexagonal building in the top left-hand corner of the garden).

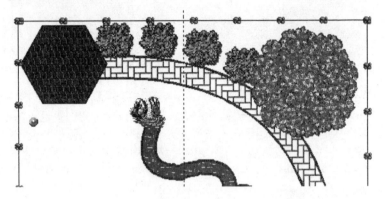

After locating the plant (**Yellow Sage** in this example) in the plant encyclopedia and clicking the **Select** button, the **Plan Objects** window appears as shown below.

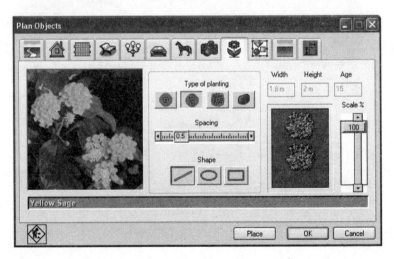

After selecting the **Type of planting** and the **Shape** (the line icon in this example) click **OK** and the plants appear on the Plan, already selected, this time including "grab" handles.

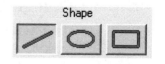

Initially the grab handles consist of small squares each containing a black circle and a white cross. At first the line of plants may be too long and contain too many plants. This can be shortened and the number of plants reduced by dragging the outer squares inwards.

Creating a Curve

The line of shrubs can be curved by dragging any of the squares in various directions until the required curve is obtained.

Moving a Line or Group of Plants

Any line or group of plants can be moved by placing the cursor over one of the plants then, while holding down the left mouse button, dragging the group of plants to the correct position.

Rotating a Line of Plants

To rotate a line of plants, click any one of the plants, as shown on the left, to select them. Then click again so that a black circle and some white circles appear, as shown below.

The line of plants can now be rotated by dragging one of the white circles. The black circle is the centre of rotation and, if necessary, this can be moved to a new position by dragging.

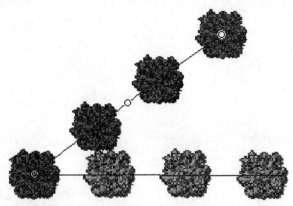

Once you have placed the plants in the correct position, at the correct angle and with curvature, if required, click anywhere outside of the plants to deselect them.

Reminder - Save Regularly

Click the **Save** icon, shown on the right, every few minutes to make sure your work isn't lost.

Planting a Flower Bed

We might now want to add a large bed containing a lot of smaller plants or flowers. This time, the plant requirements might be entered into the plant filter, e.g. white flowers, up to 0.3m (about a foot) tall, easy to care for, requiring occasional watering and quick growing. The flower might also need to be fragrant and suitable for planting in groups. When these criteria are entered into the plant filter, a list of 10 plants is found to meet the requirements, as shown below.

From this shortlist of 10 plants, we might like the look of the **Aster Dumosus 'Albus'** or **Bushy Aster 'Albus'** to use the common name. (As mentioned earlier the **Latin/ Common** button allows you to alternate between the two versions of the names). Click **Select** and you can then set up the planting arrangements for the **Asters**.

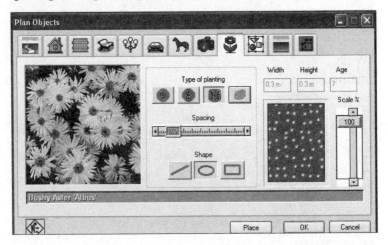

Group planting is selected under **Type of Planting** as shown on the right.

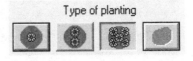

The oval/circular **Shape** is selected for the flower bed.

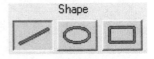

When you click **OK** the **Asters** appear on the garden design in **Plan** view in a circle as shown on the right.

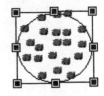

The 8 black grab handles can be used to make the shape larger or smaller, either circular or oval as shown below.

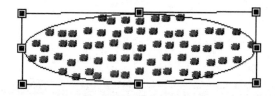

When resizing an oval/circular shape, if you want to maintain a particular shape, keep the **Shift** key held down while dragging one of the *corner* grab handles. Please note that as the size of the circle or oval is increased or decreased, the *size* of individual plants remains the same, while the *number* of plants is increased or decreased.

To rotate a bed of flowers, click over a plant so that the 8 square grab handles appear as shown above. Now click again so that 4 white circles appear. A black circle appears in the centre of the flower bed. The flower bed can now be rotated, with the black circle acting as the centre of rotation. The centre of rotation can be changed by dragging the black circle.

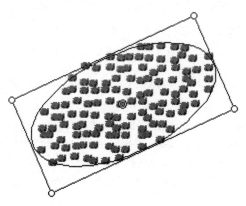

The flower bed can be moved into its final position by placing the cursor over one of the plants and dragging the entire flower bed to its new position, shown below. Click outside of the plants to deselect the flower bed.

The completed first "draft" of the garden design is shown below.

While making no claims as to the horticultural excellence of this particular garden, I hope it has demonstrated the basic steps needed to complete your own garden designs. There is still much work to be done in checking the garden design in the **3DView** and then making any changes.

Keeping Different Versions of the Garden Design

As mentioned frequently earlier in this book, it's a good idea to keep saving regularly, so that you don't lose all of your work. This can be done very simply by clicking the floppy disc icon on the Main Toolbar of the 3D Garden Designer. This quick method of saving keeps the same file name for your garden design. So if, when you first saved the design, you called it **My cottage garden**, all subsequent save operations will keep the same name. The effect of this method is to keep *overwriting* the old version of the design with the new one, on your computer's hard disc.

In the next chapter we will be looking at the garden in **3DView** and making changes. It would be useful to keep all of the different versions for comparison. These could be printed out on paper if you wanted to discuss the designs with a friend or a gardening contractor, for example. Or you could send copies of the different designs by e-mail or possibly pay a visit with the designs stored on a laptop computer.

The way to preserve all of the earlier versions of the garden design is to save the design with a new name each time. An obvious method is to use something like:

My cottage garden 1

My cottage garden 2

However, as you are allowed to use very long file names in Microsoft Windows, you could enter something more meaningful like:

My cottage garden with water feature

My tiered cottage garden

Saving the Garden Design

When the garden design is finished, click **File** and **Save As...** from the Menu Bar. The **Save As** window appears, as shown below.

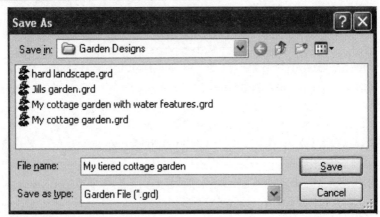

Enter the new name for the garden in the **File name** bar shown above. You needn't enter the **.grd** extension as this is added automatically. Now click the **Save** button.

If you right-click over any of the existing file names such as **hard landscape.grd** shown above, a menu appears with options including *deleting*, *copying* and *renaming* the file.

To save a file in a different location, e.g. a floppy disc, click on the arrow as shown above to the right of **Garden Designs**. More details on saving and organizing files are given in "Computing for the Older Generation", also from Bernard Babani (Publishing) Ltd (BP601).

Viewing in 3D and Editing

Introduction

The **Plan** view used in the last chapter is ideal for placing plants, hard landscaping, buildings and furniture. However, the **Plan** view doesn't give much idea of how the garden will look if you are walking around or looking out of the house, for example. The **3DView** in the Geoff Hamilton 3D Garden Designer allows you to place virtual cameras wherever you want, so that you can get a good idea of what the real garden will look like.

The cameras in the **3DView** can be moved to any position and rotated to any angle by dragging, in a similar way to the garden objects discussed earlier.

The cameras can be made to pan around the garden, simulating a leisurely stroll. It's also possible to select the month from a drop-down menu. This enables you to see the garden's various colours at different times of the year.

If there is anything you don't like - such as a shrub with the potential to grow and obscure the view from the house, this can be altered quite easily. In fact, any plant or object in the garden can be moved, replaced or deleted from the plan, as discussed shortly. As described previously, you can display both the **Plan** view and the **3DView** on the screen at the same time, in their own windows. Changes made to the **Plan** view are reflected almost immediately in the **3DView**. This makes it possible for you to develop a garden by making changes in the **Plan** view then evaluating them straightaway in the **3DView**. If you don't like working with the two windows (**Plan** view and **3DView**) on the screen at the same time, you can alternate between the two by holding down the **Alt** key and pressing the **Tab** key.

Placing Cameras

When you start a new garden design there are no cameras in place. You can still select the **3DView** by clicking on the icon on the Main Toolbar shown right or selecting **Window** and **3DView** from the menu system. The program will then give you the chance to create a camera, with the following:

A camera will be placed on the **Plan** view and this can be moved and rotated to give the required view.

You can place any number of cameras at any time in **Plan** view by selecting **Place** and **Camera**. Then the **Plan Objects** window opens as shown below.

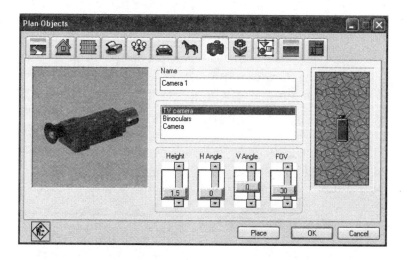

The **Name** bar in the centre allows you to delete the word **Camera 1** and replace it with a more meaningful name of your own. Underneath there is a choice between 3 different types of camera; **TV camera**, **Binoculars** and **Camera**.

TV camera   **Binoculars**   **Camera**

The **TV camera** gives a similar view to looking with the naked eye, whereas the **Binoculars** and **Camera** options give more distant and close-up shots respectively.

Underneath the three camera types are four sliders which allow you to adjust the height of a camera, the horizontal and vertical angles and the field of vision.

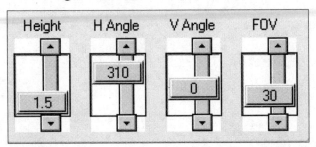

When you click **OK** the camera is placed on the **Plan**. White circles appear at each corner of the camera, shown below.

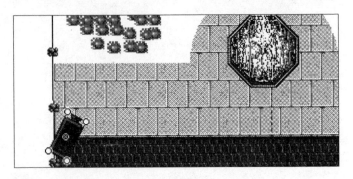

 The horizontal angle or swivel of the camera can be adjusted by dragging the white circles which appear, as shown on the left. The black circle with the white cross in the middle is the centre of rotation. This can be moved to a new position by dragging.

To move the whole camera to a new position, click anywhere on the camera (other than over the black circle) then drag to the new position.

Once a camera has been placed on the **Plan** view, you can easily change its properties by right-clicking over the camera. A menu pops up from which you select **Camera Object** and **Properties**.

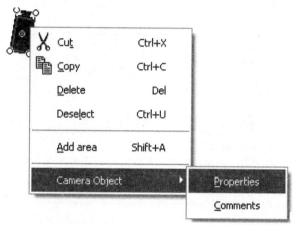

When you select **Properties**, the **Plan Objects: Camera Object Properties** window opens, allowing you to change the camera name, the type of camera, the height, the horizontal and vertical angles and the field of vision.

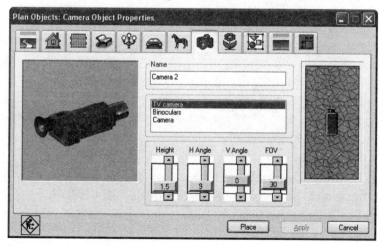

In the example below, a camera has been placed in the bottom left-hand corner of the **Plan**, to give an idea of the view from a window in the house.

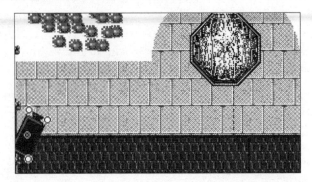

Switching to the **3DView** by clicking on the icon shown on the right on the Main Toolbar, we obtain, in this example, the image shown below.

To pan the camera around the garden, you can drag the cursor across the screen or use the four cursor "arrow" keys. Alternatively you can right-click anywhere on the **3DView** screen and select **Start rotate** from the "pop-up" menu as shown below. When you've finished your "stroll" through the virtual garden, right-click over the screen again and then select **Stop rotate** from the pop-up menu.

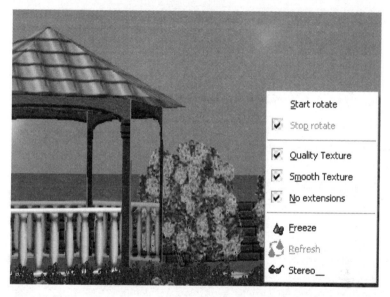

Please also note on the above menu, the **Quality Texture** and **Smooth Texture** options. These can be turned off to help the computer to work faster, but with a consequent loss of quality. With a less powerful computer, the **Freeze** option above can be used to temporarily stop the computer from constantly updating the **3DView** whenever a change is made in the **Plan** view, thus slowing the computer down. When you return to the **3DView**, click **Refresh** to update the garden with all of your changes.

The icons on the lower toolbar in **3DView** (as shown below) are different from those which appear in **Plan** view. The **3DView** icons are explained below.

 The camera icon shown on the left and on the left of the toolbar above opens up the **Plan Objects: Camera Objects Properties** window shown on page 125, allowing you to rename the camera, change the camera type, set the horizontal and vertical camera angles and alter the field of vision.

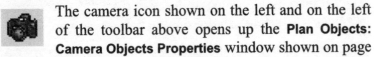 The **Sky** icon on the left (second left on the toolbar above), opens up the window shown below, giving a choice of several different skies.

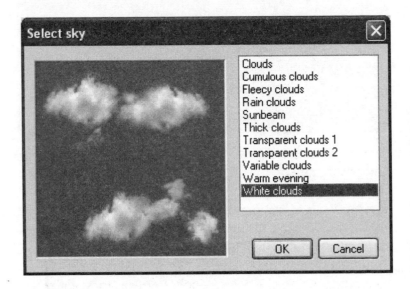

The **All colours** menu shown above is opened by clicking on the down-arrow on the right. When you select a month the colours in the garden change to match the season.

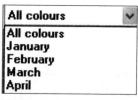

The next drop-down menu, shown under **House** in this example, lists all of the cameras you have named and placed on the garden design.

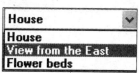

To switch to another camera click its name in the list. If you haven't entered your own names, they will be listed as **Camera 1**, **Camera 2**, etc.

The slider shown on the toolbar above and on the right allows you

to control the quality of the screen display. For high quality (but slow drawing) drag the slider to the left. For lower quality (but faster drawing) drag the slider to the right.

The next two icons select **Freeze** and **Refresh**, as discussed on page 127.

The last icon switches on **Stereo** mode, for anyone who uses stereo glasses.

You can also change cameras after selecting **View** and **Camera list...** from the Main Toolbar and opening the window shown below.

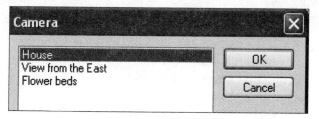

Editing a Garden Design

As mentioned previously, you can display the **3DView** and the **Plan** view on screen simultaneously. First display the **Plan** view, then switch to **3DView**. The **3DView** replaces the **Plan** view in occupying the whole screen. Now select **Window** from the Main Toolbar and the menu on the right appears. If you select **Tile Horizontal**,

the **Plan** view and **3DView** both appear on the screen in their own windows, one on top of the other as shown below.

If you prefer, select **Window** and **Tile Vertical** to display the **3DView** and the **Plan** view side-by-side as shown on the next page.

Replacing an Object in the Garden

Having studied the **3DView** you'll probably want to make some changes. All editing is done in the **Plan** view, shown on the right above. As you make changes to the **Plan** view, the **3DView** is updated. On a fast computer this will happen immediately, but there may be a few seconds delay on a slower machine, while the **3DView** is redrawn.

On looking at the **3DView** in this example, I decided that the stone in the pond was unsuitable, as shown above on the right-hand side of the **3DView** window. To change an object, double-click on the object in the **Plan** view. This opens up the **Plan Objects: Décor Object Properties** window shown on the next page. The window opens with the current object selected in the list.

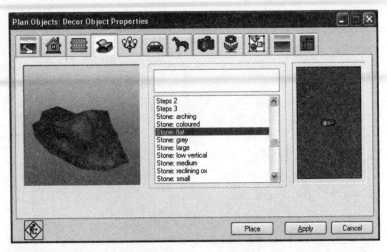

To replace the current object, in this case listed as the **Stone: v.large**, scroll through the list and select a suitable replacement. In this example **Stone: flat** is selected.

Now click **Apply** and then the **Close** icon in the top right-hand corner of the window. The replacement stone appears in the **Plan** view, selected and including "grab" handles. The new stone can be resized and moved as required. The **3DView** is updated straightaway to show the new stone.

Exactly the same method is used to change the other garden objects, such as the paved surface areas, i.e.

- Double-click on the object
- Select the replacement in the **Plan Objects** window.
- Click the **Apply** button and the **Close** icon.
- Adjust the size and move to its final position.
- Finally click outside of the object to deselect it, removing the red highlighting and the grab handles.

Resizing an Object

Select the object in the **Plan** view by clicking over it, e.g. the Water Fountain on the patio in the sample garden design, shown on the right. The selected object is highlighted in red with eight black squares or "grab" handles around its perimeter. Drag any of the black squares to make the object bigger or smaller. Click outside of the object to deselect it, i.e. remove the red highlighting and the grab handles.

Moving an Object

Select the object by clicking over it then keep the left-hand mouse button held down. The cursor should change to a man with a load on his back. Drag the object to its new position before deselecting it by clicking outside.

Rotating an Object

Select the object so that eight black squares appear as shown above. Now click again to produce four white circles as shown on the right. The object can now be rotated by dragging any of the circles. Deselect the object by clicking anywhere outside of it.

Deleting an Object

To remove an object altogether, select the object then press the **Delete** key.

Copying an Object

To copy an object, hold down the **Ctrl** key while dragging the duplicate copy to its new position. Deselect the object.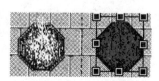

Please note that many of the previous editing tasks on an existing garden can be carried out after right-clicking over the object in the **Plan** view. The following menu appears.

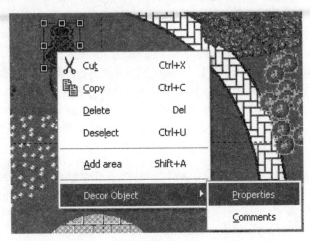

If you select **Properties** as shown above, the **Plan Objects** window opens, as shown on page 132, allowing you to replace the selected object. If the selected object is a fence, you can change the type of fencing, the height, shape, the panel size or space between posts.

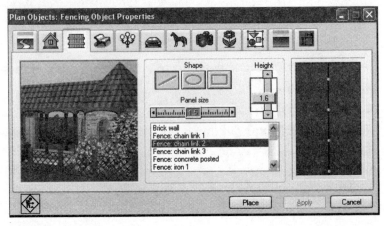

Editing Plants

Many of the editing operations just described for objects such as water features, buildings, paths and hard landscaping in general can also be carried out on plants. A bed of plants arranged in an oval, circle, square or rectangle can be made bigger or smaller by dragging the grab handles. Plants can be moved by dragging to their new position. You can delete a plant by selecting it then pressing the **Delete** key. Several editing operations are available after right-clicking over the plant in the **Plan** view. The following menus appear.

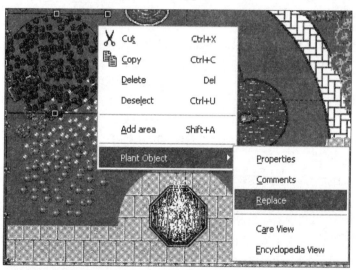

Replacing Plants

Now select **Plant Object** and **Replace** and the built-in plant encyclopedia opens, allowing you to find a replacement plant. After clicking the **Select** button at the bottom of the plant encyclopedia, the **Plan Objects** window opens as shown on the next page.

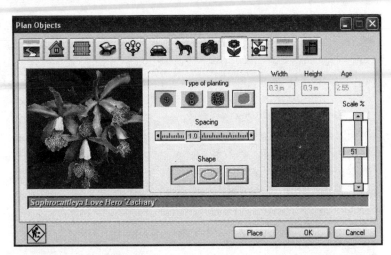

As described earlier, the **Plan Objects** window allows you to set the planting arrangements, such as singly or in groups, also the spacing between plants and whether they will be planted in circles, ovals, rectangles, etc. The sliding scale is used to set the age of the plant at the time of planting. When you click **OK** the newly selected plants replace the old ones on the garden **Plan**.

Saving the Finished Design

When you have finished editing the garden you need to save the design as a file on your hard disc. To keep the same name, click the disc icon on the Main Toolbar. To save with a different

name click **File** and **Save As...** and enter the new name, as described on page 119. You might also make a backup copy on a separate medium such as a floppy disc, by selecting the disc in the **Save As** window, as shown below.

Adding Some Finishing Touches

When you've finished the hard landscaping and planting, you may wish to add some additional features. The Geoff Hamilton 3D Garden Designer provides a host of extra features accessed by selecting **Place** on the Menu Bar. These are placed on the **Plan** view, then moved and rotated in a similar way to the hard

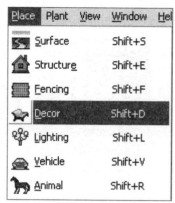

landscaping objects described in Chapter 5. However, since these objects are drawn to scale, they cannot be resized.

The **Décor** menu presents a vast range of objects such as tables and chairs, barbecue, climbing frame, bridges, bird tables, clothes driers, water features, steps, sculptures, paddling pool, satellite dish and plants in containers.

The **Vehicle** menu contains every type of vehicle likely to be kept in a domestic garden, including cars, bicycles, lawnmowers, motorcycles, a trailer and boats.

The **Animals** menu includes a range of domestic animals and birds. For anyone with a larger garden or smallholding there are also several farm animals.

Finally the **Lighting** menu allows you to place five different types of lantern in the garden. You can select the height of the lantern and the power in a range from 20 to 1000 watts.

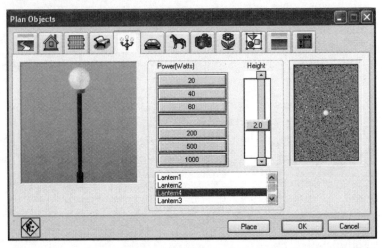

When you place a lantern in the garden in **Plan** view and select the **Night-time** view using the **Plan Toolbar** icon shown on the right, the spread of the lighting is shown as an illuminated circle.

Printing and Sending Garden Designs

Introduction

When the garden design is complete and you've done any necessary editing, you may want to make some printouts on paper. You can print copies of both the **Plan** view and the **3DView**. A copy of the monthly care and maintenance schedules for the plants chosen for your particular garden can also be printed.

Printouts on paper are useful if you want to study the design away from your computer, perhaps with a gardening contractor or supplier or with a friend who doesn't have a computer. Alternatively, if you have a laptop computer, this could also be used for displaying your designs away from home. If your acquaintances have their own computer system with the Geoff Hamilton 3D Garden Designer software installed, then you could send them a copy of the garden design by e-mail. Another option would be to place a copy of the garden design on a CD, ZIP disc, floppy disc, etc., and send it to them in the ordinary post. These various alternatives are discussed in the remainder of this chapter.

Inkjet Colour Printers

To display your garden designs on paper you need a colour printer and this generally means an *inkjet*. There is a now a wide choice of such printers capable of producing excellent colour printouts and costing anything from £30 to £200 or more. Well-known manufacturers of inkjet printers are firms such as Epson, Hewlett Packard, Canon and Lexmark. An Epson Stylus inkjet printer is shown below.

While an inkjet printer can now be bought for as little as £30, the combined cost of the black and colour cartridges for some printers may be nearer £50. One solution is to buy cheaper *compatible* or *remanufactured* cartridges from third party suppliers. Not surprisingly, manufacturers of the genuine article have expressed doubts about the cheaper alternative cartridges.

An inkjet printer will also be useful if you have a digital camera and want to print photographs to record your real garden at different stages of its development.

Digital photography is an excellent aid to garden design and development; if you would like more information on the subject you might be interested in reading "Digital Photography and Computing for the Older Generation" from Bernard Babani (publishing) Ltd.

Printing a Garden Design

The method of printing from the 3D Garden Designer is the same in both **Plan** view and **3DView**.

With the 3D Garden Designer program running and displaying your chosen garden design on the screen, click **File** and **Print...** from the menus. Alternatively click the **Print** icon on the Main Toolbar, shown on the right. The **Garden Print** window opens, as shown below.

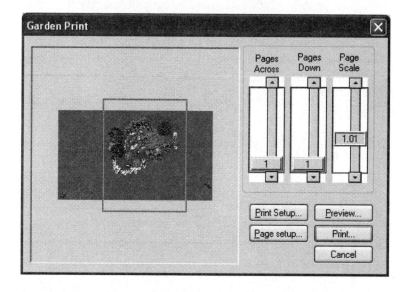

The panel on the left shows a miniature plan view of the garden, enclosed by a frame representing the edges of the paper. The frame can be moved by dragging.

The **Page Scale** slider shown on the right above allows you to alter the size of the garden design in relation to the paper. The highest setting will show a small image in the middle of the paper.

The **Pages Across** and **Pages Down** sliders allow a large garden design to be spread over a number of pages.

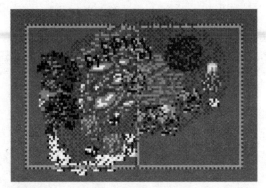

The **Page Setup...** button shown on page 141 allows you to add a header and footer as shown below and also to set the margins. Radio buttons, shown below, allow the display of guide lines and rulers to be switched on and off.

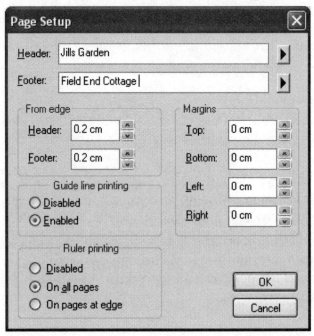

The **Print Setup...** button shown on page 141 opens the **Print Setup** window shown below. The **Print Setup** window can also be launched by clicking **File** and **Print Setup...** from the 3D Garden Designer Menu Bar.

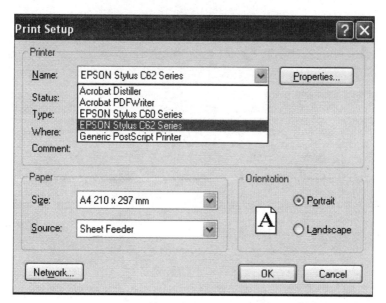

The **Print Setup** window allows you to choose the paper size and set the paper orientation as either **Portrait** or **Landscape**, as shown above and on the right.

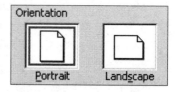

The **Print Setup...**window also allows you to select the printer to be used, if more than one device is available.

Clicking the **Properties...** button shown above launches the **Properties** window for your particular model of printer. Shown on the next page is the **Properties** window for an Epson Stylus printer.

The three tabs **Main, Page Layout** and **Maintenance** give access to a large number of printer settings, such as the quality and speed of printing and the use of black and/or coloured ink. The **Main** tab also indicates the amount of black and coloured ink remaining in the cartridges.

If you click the **Maintenance** tab shown above, another window appears, as shown on the next page, presenting several options including checking the ink cartridges and cleaning the print head nozzles on the Epson printer.

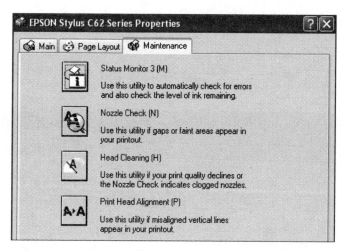

The **Preview...** button shown on page 141 enables you to check the print setup, as shown below, before committing it to paper.

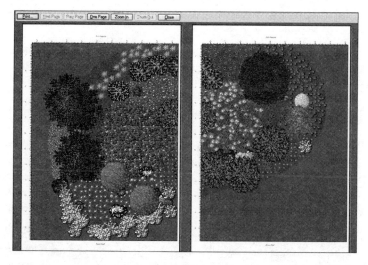

Finally, when you are happy with the **Preview**, click the **Print...** button to copy the garden design onto paper.

Printing Care and Maintenance Information

The Geoff Hamilton 3D Garden Designer has a built-in **Care** feature which will still be useful after the real garden has been created. Click on **Window** and **Care** and a table appears as shown below.

Plant total	Name		April			
2	Clematis 'Comtesse de Bouchaud'	🐦 🪴	⟋			
6	Clematis 'Jackmanii'	🐦 🪴	⟋			
2	Clematis 'Proteus'	🐦 🪴	⟋			
6	Common Cat's-Tail	𝕀 🪴 🐦	⟋ ✿ ❀			
48	Common Sword Lily	𝕀 🧴	⟋ ⟋ 🐦			

The table relates only to the plants in the selected garden design. The first two columns list the names of the plants and the number of each variety in the garden. The remainder of the table consists of columns for each month. Each row across the table displays the care and maintenance tasks for a particular type of plant, for each month of the year. The tasks are represented by icons, as shown below.

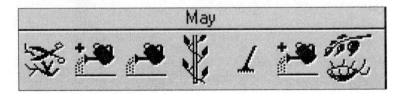

You can scroll through the different months and plants using the four cursor or arrow keys. If you are not sure what a particular care icon means, click on the icon to obtain a complete description. For example, clicking on the icon shown on the right produces the following description of **Rhizome division**.

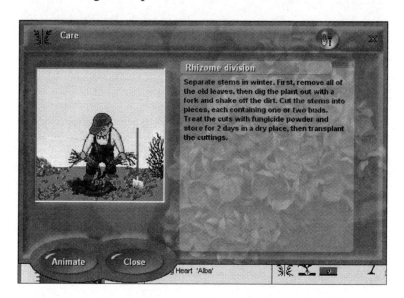

Clicking the **Animate** button shown above produces a step-by-step video demonstration of the selected task. The **Care** table can be printed out on paper using **File** and **Print....** from the Menu Bar. Then it can be used away from the computer as a schedule of what tasks need to be done throughout the year in your particular garden.

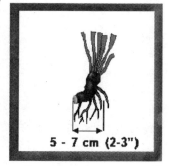

Printing Your Own Notes

You can keep notes about the garden as a whole by selecting **Window** and **Notes** from the 3D Garden Designer Menu Bar. Then type your notes on the blank sheet.

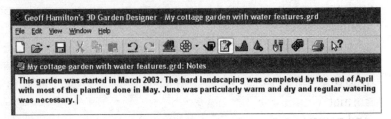

When you save a garden design the notes are saved with it. If you want to add some notes about an individual plant or object in your garden, right-click over the object and select **Plant Object** (or **Structure Object**, etc.) and then **Comments.**

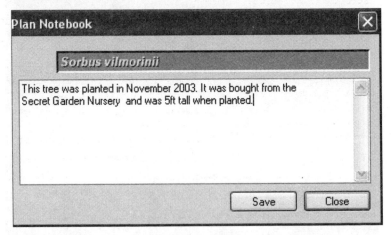

To print your notes, select (i.e. mark or highlight) the text with the mouse, then right-click over the text and select **Copy** from the pop-up menu. Then switch to a word processor such as Word or Notepad. **Paste** the text onto the page and select **File** and **Print...** to print the notes on paper.

E-mailing a Garden Design

This is a quick and easy way to send a copy of a garden design to a friend or acquaintance anywhere in the world. It only takes a few seconds and the recipient can see the design as soon as they read their e-mail. For your friend or contact to view the garden design after e-mailing, their computer must have the Geoff Hamilton 3D Garden Designer software installed. As discussed later, it is also possible to convert the garden design file to the .JPG format which can be viewed on lots of different drawing and painting programs.

The 3D Garden Designer has its own e-mail option included in the **File** menu. First start the 3D Garden Designer and open the required garden design on the screen. Now select **File** and **Send...** from the Menu Bar. This launches the e-mail program installed on your computer, such as Outlook Express, as shown below.

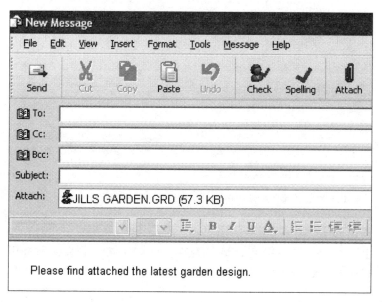

As shown on the previous page, the computer has already entered the file name for the garden design, listed next to **Attach**. Enter the e-mail address of your contact in the **To:** slot and type a **Subject** and a covering message before clicking the **Send** button. You can test the above method by sending an e-mail (together with a garden design) to yourself as the recipient. When the e-mail is received in the inbox, the recipient double-clicks the file name next to **Attachment** as shown below.

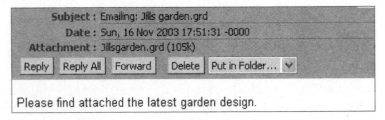

The file will then be downloaded and saved in a folder chosen by the recipient, such as **C:\Download files** below.

The recipient now double-clicks the name or icon for the downloaded file. The 3D Garden Designer will start up, displaying the garden design. (The recipient's computer must have the 3D Garden Designer software installed and the CD must be present in the CD-Drive.)

Using Send To in Microsoft Windows

Microsoft Windows has a built-in **Send To** option to send a copy of a file to various destinations. These destinations include e-mail recipients, other folders on your hard disc and also removable magnetic storage media such as floppy discs, CDs, ZIP discs and memory cards.

First it is necessary to display the file for your garden design in the Windows Explorer. Right-click over the *start* button then click **Explore** and browse to the folder where your garden designs have been saved. Icons and file names for your designs should be displayed as shown below. In this example, a design called **Jills garden.grd** is stored in the folder **Garden Designs** on my **C:** drive. The full path name of this garden design is therefore:

C:\Garden Designs\Jills garden.grd

The file name and icon are shown below in the Windows Explorer.

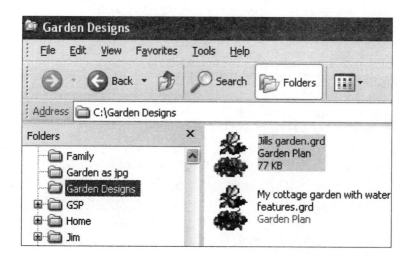

Sending a Design to a Separate Disc or Storage Device

It may be convenient to copy a garden design to a separate magnetic disc, such as a floppy disc, recordable CD (CD-R or CD-RW) or a ZIP disc. This will enable the design to be viewed on another computer, perhaps after sending the disc through the conventional post. First you need to open the folder containing your garden designs in the Windows Explorer as discussed on page 151. Right-click over the file name or icon for the chosen garden design and select **Send To** from the menu, as shown below.

Now select the destination for the garden design to be copied to. In this example, we could use the **3½ Floppy (A:)**, the **CD Drive(D:)** or the **SmartMedia(E:)** card.

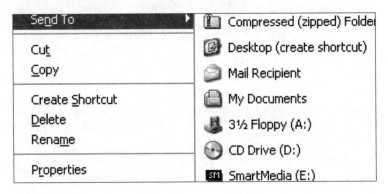

If you have another sort of removable magnetic storage medium such as a ZIP disc, this should appear automatically in the **Send To** menu shown above. The person receiving the disc can transfer the file to the **My Documents** folder on their hard disc by starting the Windows Explorer and right-clicking over the file, to launch the **Send To** menu shown above.

Using Export in the 3D Garden Designer

The 3D Garden Designer provides an option to export various sets of information from a garden design, to different destinations. The destination might be another folder on your hard disc or a different medium such as a floppy disc. Click **File** and **Export...** from the 3D Garden Designer Menu Bar to start the process.

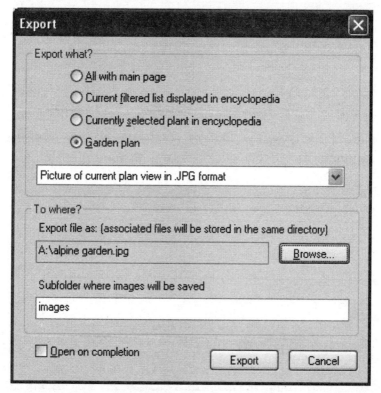

If you switch on the radio button next to **Garden plan** on the **Export** dialogue box shown on the previous page, the bar changes to show **Picture of current plan view in .JPG format** as shown above.

.JPG is a file format which is compatible with many different drawing and painting programs such as Microsoft Paint. So if you save a garden design in this format and send it to someone else, they could view the design without having the 3D Garden Designer installed on their computer. (Garden designs are normally saved in the 3D Garden Designer using the special **.grd** file format).

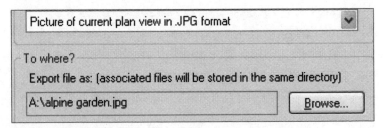

Next click **Browse...** to select the destination for the exported file and then click **Save** and **Export** to finish.

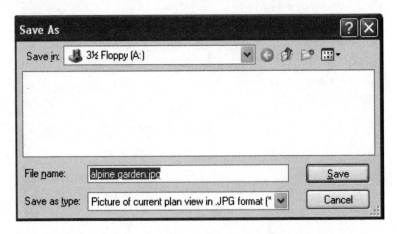

Geoff Hamilton's Plant Encyclopedia

Introduction

Geoff Hamilton's Plant Encyclopedia CD-ROM is a companion to the 3D Garden Designer program on which this book is based. It is supplied as a stand-alone program on a separate CD, although both programs may be obtained together as a limited edition boxed set.

The main features of the Plant Encyclopedia include:

- Details of over 4000 plants, trees and shrubs.
- Advice on care and maintenance.
- Advanced searches tailored to match your personal requirements and local garden conditions.
- High quality colour photographs of every plant.
- Suggestions for additional plants which will complement your chosen plants if planted together.
- Slide shows of your selected plants.
- Printed lists of chosen plants, useful when visiting the garden centre or ordering plants.
- Well-designed menus and screen displays which make the program powerful, yet very easy to use.

Installing the Plant Encyclopedia

As with most software, it's simply a case of placing the CD in the drive and following the instructions on the screen. Then you need to supply some personal details and register your purchase of the software. Next click **Start Program** as shown on the previous page to start the **InstallShield Wizard**. The wizard mainly involves clicking **Next** and accepting the settings provided by the program. You may have to enter your name and organization (if applicable).

You will be asked to choose the type of installation. Most users should accept the **Typical** setup, so that all program features are installed. If you are worried about your hard disc space being low then select the **Minimal** radio button. Click **Next** and the files should be copied to your hard disc. Finally click **Finish** to complete the installation process.

Starting the Plant Encyclopedia

The installation process will have placed an icon on the Windows Desktop, as shown on the right. Double-click this icon to start the program. Alternatively you can use the Windows menus by clicking **start**, **All Programs**, **Plant Encyclopedia** and **Geoff Hamilton's Plant Encyclopedia** as shown below.

Please Note: In order to run the Plant Encyclopedia the CD-ROM must always be present in the CD drive.

Displaying Plant Information

The main window for displaying plant information is displayed as soon as the plant encyclopedia starts up.

Initially the "selection" comprises all 4027 plants in the Plant Encyclopedia (displayed in alphabetical order) as indicated in the title bar shown enlarged below.

> 🖳 Geoff Hamilton's Plant Encyclopedia [Plant 847 of 4027]

The main Plant Encyclopedia window shown on the previous page will also be used to display the reduced lists of plants after searching operations, discussed later in this chapter. Searching for plants meeting certain criteria will result in a smaller number than **4027** being displayed in the title bar above. For example, after searching for all plants having red flowers, the number **4027** is replaced by **421**.

The right-hand panel on the main Plant Encyclopedia window on page 157 is headed by the plant's common and Latin names. Underneath is a detailed description of the plant. The description also includes plants which can be grown successfully "in harmony" with the selected plant. These plants are highlighted in blue and the names can be clicked to obtain more details of the "companion" plants.

The lower part of the right-hand panel gives details of the cultivation of the plant. Finally in the right-hand panel shown on page 157, there are details such as the plant type, the type of soil it can tolerate, its hardiness, the original source of the plant species and the date and source of the main photograph.

Type:	Trees	pH:	Acid
Themes:	Attractive to wildlife		
Soil Type:	Loam, Clay		
Attributes:			

Hardiness zone: 3
Origin: Garden - USA 1896
Photo: Hilliers Arboretum, Hants, 5 Oct

Scrolling through the Plants

The scroll bar at the bottom of the Plant Encyclopedia is shown below.

The scroll bar can be used in 3 different ways.

- To move through the plants one at a time, click the arrows on the left and right ends of the scroll bar.

- To move through the plants in steps of approximately 10% of the currently selected list, click either side of the slider or "thumb" in the scroll bar track.

- To scroll through the currently selected list of plants, drag the slider or thumb.

The Plant Icons

As shown below, the height and spread of each plant is displayed in metres. As discussed shortly, you can change these measurements to Imperial units (feet and inches).

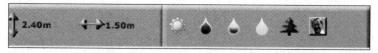

The group of icons shown on the right above varies in number and type from plant to plant, depending on the plant's individual preferences and characteristics. Icons represent plant properties such as tolerance to dry, moist and wet soil and full sun, partial shade and shade. Other icons represent evergreen trees, plants grown or written about by Geoff Hamilton, plants which might be dangerous to children, toxic, prickly or harmful to the skin. These icons are discussed in more detail shortly in the section on searching for plants meeting certain criteria.

The group of icons in the bottom right of the Plant Encyclopedia shows the months when a plant flowers, has significant leaf interest and has significant fruit interest.

Click each of the icons (shown on the left above) in turn to highlight the best months for flowers, leaf display and fruit. Please note that within the database of 4027 plants, some plants will display none of the above flower, leaf and fruit icons while others may only display one or two.

The Main Menu

On the top left of the main Plant Encyclopedia window, the garden shed icon (shown right) launches the drop-down menu shown below.

The **Help** button shown on the right leads to an on-screen manual including links to a Web site giving technical support. You can carry out a quick search for a plant by typing its name into the blank space next to the magnifying glass. Capital and lower case letters are equally acceptable and you need only enter the first few letters of a plant's name. This may result in some unwanted plants being added to the list. For example, entering **Pine** will find **Pineapple** as well as the **Mountain pine**, etc. Both common names and Latin names may be entered.

Searching for Plants

Clicking the **Search** button on the drop-down menu shown on the previous page launches the main search window shown below. You can enter a name for the plant and/or any combination of other criteria selected from the list below. Obviously the more criteria you enter, the smaller will be the resulting list of matching plants.

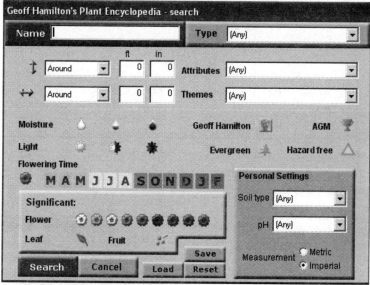

Clicking the arrow to the right of **Type** presents a drop-down menu allowing you to select the plant type as shown below. Other types such as **Herbaceous**, **Palms**, **Shrubs** and **Trees** can be selected after scrolling down the menu.

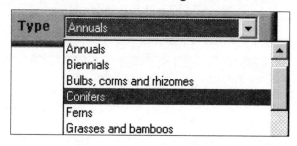

The plant height and spread can be specified using drop-down menus, as shown below. Plants can be found which are **Around, Less than** or **Greater than** the measurements entered in the boxes on the right.

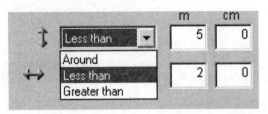

If you prefer to work in feet and inches, switch on **Imperial** under **Personal Settings** in the

bottom right of the search window shown on page 161.

Attributes and **Themes** on the right of the search window provide two drop-down menus giving additional plant properties which may be entered into the search.

Attributes   **Themes**

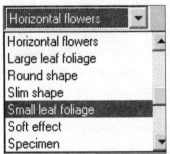   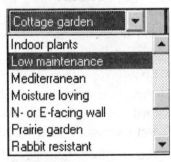

The complete lists of **Attributes** and **Themes** can be viewed by scrolling up or down the menus using the scroll bars on the right of each window shown above.

Two sets of icons in the centre left of the search window shown on page 161 allow you to search for plants which will tolerate different levels of **Moisture** and **Light**, to suit the conditions in the intended situation in your garden.

The icons for **Moisture** represent, from left to right, well-drained, moist and wet soil. The **Light** icons specify full sun, partial shade and full shade. In each case, you can select one or two of the three criteria.

A group of four icons occupying the centre right of the search window on page 161 are shown below.

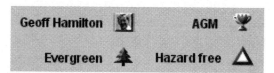

If you select the **Geoff Hamilton** icon above, the search will find plants which Geoff Hamilton wrote about or included in his garden at Barnsdale.

Clicking on **AGM** will find plants that have received the Award of Garden Merit from the Royal Horticultural Society, given to plants of proven all-round excellence.

If you select the **Evergreen** icon, the search will be limited to the **707** evergreen plants in the encyclopedia's database.

The **Hazard free** icon excludes from the search results plants which are toxic, thorny or can cause irritation. Users are advised that other plants may have harmful features.

The next group of icons in the lower left of the search window shown on page 161 allows you to select plants according to their flowers and any leaf or fruit qualities.

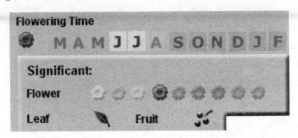

Under **Flowering Time** shown above, select one or more months to search for plants flowering at that time. Under **Significant: Flower** select one or more colours for the flowers you wish to find. Clicking the **Leaf** and **Fruit** icons will find plants which are notable in these respects, e.g., for autumn leaves and for attractive berries and fruit.

The **Personal Settings** on the bottom right of the search window allow you to specify your own soil conditions. Clicking the down arrow to the right of **Soil type** presents the choice shown on the left below. The **pH** drop-down menu gives a choice of soils

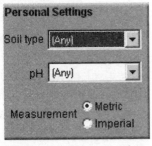

between **Acid**, (pH less than 7.0), **Alkaline** (pH more than 7.0) and **Neutral** (pH value equal to 7.0).

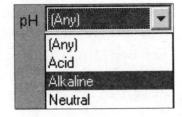

When you've finished entering all of your search criteria, click the **Search** button at the bottom of the search window.

The screen will now present the main Plant Encyclopedia, but this will only display those plants that match your search criteria. You can browse through this restricted list as described earlier in this chapter. The **Save** button above enables you to save the criteria for this particular search, with a title of your choice. This search can be retrieved at a later date using the **Load** button shown above. The **Reset** button above clears the current search criteria.

Other Main Menu Options

Let's now return to the menu displayed after clicking the garden shed icon shown on the right and on the main Plant Encyclopedia screen on page 157.

View all changes the current plant selection from the results of any search to a display of the entire collection of 4027 plants in the encyclopedia.

Print makes a paper copy of the plant photograph and all of the descriptive information.

About gives details about the design and production of the program, also contributors and technical support.

Exit closes the program.

Pick lists and **Slide show** are discussed on the next two pages.

Pick Lists

This feature allows you to compile a list of plants, perhaps as a record of every plant in your garden or as a shopping list of plants you want to obtain. Pick lists can be saved and viewed at later date. They can also be printed on paper. Plants are added to a pick list when the main plant encyclopedia screen is displaying either a selection of plants or the full list of 4027 plants in the encyclopedia. To

add the currently displayed plant to a pick list, simply click the icon next to the garden shed icon. A tick appears as shown on the right. Repeat this process
for every plant you wish to include in the pick list.

To display the pick list, click the garden shed icon and select **Pick lists** from the drop-down menu shown on the previous page.

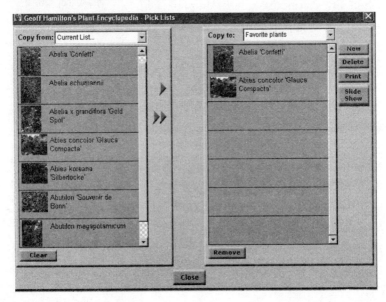

The newly ticked or "bookmarked" plants appear in the **Current List** in the left-hand panel shown on the previous page. The **Current List** can be emptied using the **Clear** button. Individual plants can be selected in the **Current List** and copied to a pick list in the right-hand panel by clicking the single arrow in the middle. Click the double arrow to copy all of the plants from the **Current List** to the pick list in the right-hand panel.

New pick lists can be created and saved with their own name, in the right-hand panel shown below and on the previous page. Existing pick lists can be selected from the drop-down menu shown on the right below.

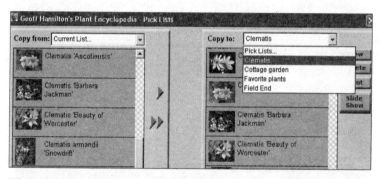

The names of plants displayed in a pick list in the right-hand panel can be printed on paper using the **Print** button on the right side of the right-hand panel. There is also a **New** button to create a new pick list, **Delete** to remove the selected list and **Slide Show** to create a continuous display of the plants in the pick list.

The **Remove** button at the bottom of the right-hand panel shown on the previous page is used to delete individual plants selected in the pick list.

Slide Show

You can run a slide show of the plants in a pick list using the **Slide Show** button shown on the previous page. A slide show can also be run after a search, using the **Slide Show** option on the main menu shown on page 165.

Apart from the normal **Play** and **Stop** buttons shown above, a continuously revolving slide show can be set up using **Loop** and a suitable display time in seconds.

Appendix 1: Dealing with Sloping Ground

The Geoff Hamilton 3D Garden Designer has a landscape feature which allows you to take account of sloping ground in your designs. This is a little more complicated than most of the other topics described in this book, by necessity involving some trigonometry. As this topic may bring back unhappy memories from school days for some people, it has been placed in this appendix where it can more easily be ignored, if preferred.

Calculating the Slope of the Garden

Place a stake at the highest part of the garden and tie a length of string to it. Extend the string along the length of the slope and, with the help of an assistant, makes sure the string is pulled tight and kept level using a spirit level. Measure the length of string **d** and the height above the ground **h**, as shown below.

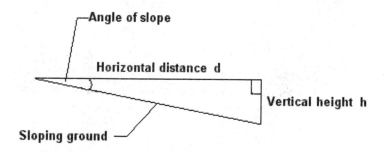

From the above diagram,

Angle of slope= inv-Tan(h/d)

This can be worked out on a calculator such as the on-screen calculator in Microsoft Windows, found in **All Programs/Accessories**. Select **View/Scientific** and **Degrees**.

Sample Calculation	Example
Enter the height **h** metres	2.9
Click divide "/" and enter the distance **d** metres	10.7
Click **=**	0.2710
Click the **Inv** box at the top of the calculator.	
Click the **tan** button	
Angle of slope of the garden in degrees	15.16

This slope can be included in the garden design in **Landscape** view as discussed shortly.

Direction of Slope

This is the angle measured between the direction of the slope and a line measured up the garden or up the screen, as discussed earlier. One length of string is placed in the up screen direction. Another piece of string of equal length to the first is placed from the end of the first piece of string, in the upward direction of the slope. The angle between the strings can be measured directly with a protractor.

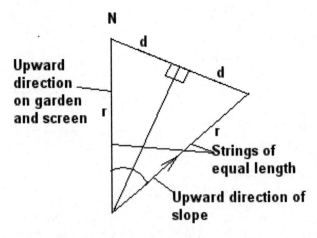

Alternatively the angle can be calculated using:

Angle = 2 x inv-Sin (d/r)

Sample Calculation	**Example**
Enter the distance **d** metres	7.1
Click divide "*/*" and enter the length of string **r**	25.9
Click **=**	0.2741
Click the **Inv** box at the top of the calculator	
Click the **sin** button	15.91
Click multiply "**x**"	
Click **2** and **=**	31.82

This is the angle in degrees between the upward direction of the slope and the upward direction of the whole garden.

Applying Raised or Sunken Points to a Garden Design

The **Landscape** view is used for all work involving slopes and raised levels, hillocks and dips, etc.

With the garden design open in the **Plan** view, select the **Landscape** view using the icon on the Main Toolbar as shown on the right.

The **Tools** menu in **Landscape** view allows you to add points, i.e. small hillocks or dips. Click **Select/add points** as shown below on the left. The height of the hillock can be specified and the shape adjusted using the slider shown on the right below.

Adding Sloping and Raised Areas

To specify a sloping area in **Landscape** view you must first click **Select Area** on the menu shown previously then click on the area to select it. Then click **Tools** and **Select area properties**.

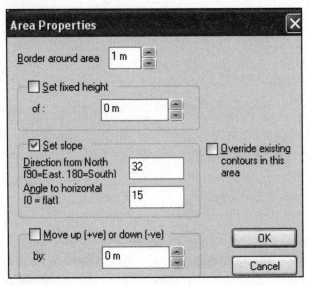

Now click **Set slope** so that a tick appears. First you set the upward direction of the slope measured from North, an angle between 0 and 360 degrees. This was calculated earlier in the example as 31.8 degrees. You then enter the angle of the slope relative to the horizontal – calculated earlier in the example as 15.16 degrees. Click **OK** to create the slope in the garden design. To see the effect of these changes switch to **3DView** by clicking its icon on the Main Toolbar, as shown on the right.

As shown above, there are options to raise areas to a fixed height and also to move them up or down by a fixed amount.

Appendix 2: Computer Requirements

Listed below are the minimum computer requirements for running the three Geoff Hamilton software packages, namely Garden Designer, 3D Garden Designer and Plant Encyclopedia. If your computer doesn't meet the specification listed for a particular package, the program may still function but the speed of operation may be slow.

Garden Designer	3D Garden Designer	Plant Encyclopedia
IBM PC compatible	IBM PC compatible	IBM PC compatible
486 processor	200MHz processor	100MHz processor
4MB RAM	32MB RAM	32MB RAM
2MB Hard disc space	30MB Hard disc space	Not critical
Windows 95, 98 or XP	Windows 95, 98, 2000 or XP	Windows 95, 98, Me, 2000 or XP.
256 colour screen	16 bit colour 800x600 screen	16 bit colour 1024x768 screen
CD ROM drive	CD ROM drive	CD ROM drive
Colour printer	Colour printer	Colour Printer

The above table, by necessity, uses quite a lot of computing jargon. If you're not sure what any of the terms mean, they are explained on the following pages. There is also help in finding out the technical specification of your particular computer in relation to the above requirements.

IBM PC Compatible Computer

This is the standard with which most new computers comply, enabling them all to run the same software, usually under a version of the Microsoft Windows operating system. Unless you buy an Apple Macintosh, any new computer will almost certainly be an IBM PC compatible.

Processor

This is the microchip which acts as the "brains" of the computer - carrying out millions of instructions and calculations per second. The number in MHz (*megahertz*), e.g. 200MHz, refers to the speed of the processor. If your computer was bought new in recent years, the processor should comfortably exceed the requirements listed in the table on the previous page.

RAM

The RAM is the *memory* of the computer, used to store temporarily the current program and data. The RAM is cleared when the computer is switched off. The size of the RAM is stated in *megabytes* or MB for short. 1MB is the amount of memory needed to store roughly 1 million characters, such as letters of the alphabet or the digits 0,1,2,3,4,5,6,7,8,9. Computers are currently supplied with typical RAM sizes of 128MB, 256MB or 512MB.

Hard Disc Space

The hard disc drive is a set of magnetic discs inside of the computer, on which programs and data are permanently saved or recorded. Eventually the hard disc fills up and there may not be enough space to record new programs. Hard disc space was originally measured in megabytes, but the latest hard discs are so large they are quoted in *gigabytes* or GB for short. 1GB is roughly 1000MB.

To find the amount of free hard disc space available on a computer running Windows XP, select **start** and **My Computer** and allow the mouse cursor to hover over the icon for your hard disc (usually called the **C:** drive). A small label appears showing that, in the computer used in this example, there is a free space of 12GB out of a total capacity

of 19GB. Currently computers are supplied with typical hard disc sizes of 20, 40 and 80GB.

CD ROM Drive

A CD ROM drive is essential for the initial installation of the software. The original software CD must also be *present in the CD drive* whenever you run the garden designer software or the plant encyclopedia. If your computer doesn't have a CD ROM drive fitted, any local computer shop should be able to install one in a few minutes. You need to buy a drive designated *CD-RW*, as this can also *write* information onto a blank CD as well as read from a CD containing information. CD-RW drives currently cost from about £40 upwards, but buy the best you can afford in order to keep up with the latest developments.

Screen Colours and Resolution

This information can be checked in Windows XP by selecting *start*, **Control Panel** and double-clicking the **Display** icon  as shown on the right. Then click the **Settings** tab in the **Display Properties** window as shown below.

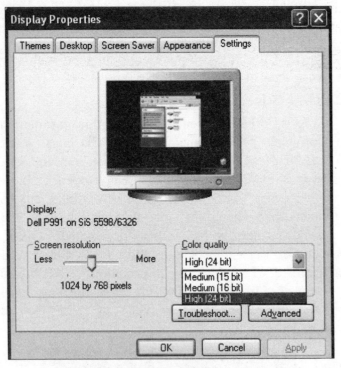

The screen resolution is the number of small squares or *picture elements* (pixels) used to map out the screen. This particular computer has a screen resolution of **1024 by 768 pixels,** set using the adjustable slider shown under **Screen resolution** above. **24 bit** colour has been selected from the drop-down menu shown above under **Color quality**.

Finding More Details

You can find more of the details of your computer's specification in Windows XP by selecting *start*, **Control Panel** and double-clicking the **System** icon as shown on the right. The **System Properties** window should appear and with the **General** tab selected, you will see a number of details about your computer's specification.

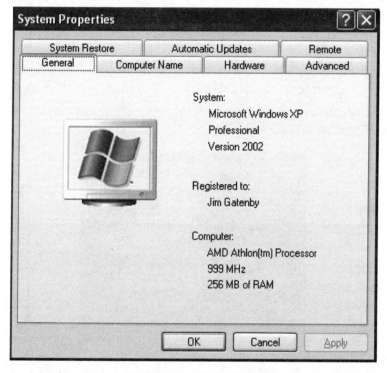

As can be seen above, this particular computer is running **Microsoft Windows XP Professional**. The processor speed is **999MHz** and there is **256MB of RAM** - ample power to run the Geoff Hamilton software.

Windows 95, 98, Me, 2000 or XP

These are various versions of the Microsoft Windows *operating system*, used to control many of the tasks carried out by the computer. These tasks include controlling the screen display and the various menus used to run programs and carry out operations such as saving and printing documents.

Microsoft Windows is designed to be easy to use, with many tasks being carried out by using a *mouse* to move a cursor about the screen, pointing and clicking at icons and menu items to initiate operations. The term "Windows" derives from the small rectangular boxes used to display the current program and to present information to the user.

Most computers are now supplied with the latest version of Windows, known as Windows XP.

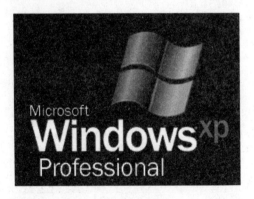

Colour Printer

This is essential for getting the most out of Geoff Hamilton's 3D Garden Designer and Geoff Hamilton's Plant Encyclopedia. Colour printers are discussed in Chapter 9, Printing and Sending Garden Designs.

Index

Special Offer on Geoff Hamilton Software

Readers of this book are entitled to buy the best selling 3D Garden Designer software at half the normal retail price, as follows:

Geoff Hamilton 3D Garden Designer

Recommended Retail Price	£19.99
Special Buy Price	£9.99

Geoff Hamilton Plant Encyclopedia

Recommended Retail Price	£9.99
Special Buy Price	£4.99
Postage and Packaging	£3.00

(Total postage if one or both titles purchased)

Purchasing via the Internet

To purchase the software via the Internet, please visit the Web site at:

www.gsp.cc/specialoffers

Password: **Geoff**

E-mail: **cserv@gsp.cc**

Purchasing by Post

Please fill in the order form over the page (or a copy of it) and post it with your payment details to:

GSP Customer Services/Gardening offer
Freepost (PE717)
Meadow Lane
S. Ives
Cambs
PE27 4BR

The author and publishers of this book accept no responsibility for the supply, quality or magnetic contents of the compact discs, or in respect of any damage or injury that might be suffered or caused by their use. This offer may be subject to alteration or withdrawal without further notice.

Payment Information

Title [   ] Initials [   ] Surname [   ]

Address [   ]

Postcode [   ] Email [   ]

Daytime Telephone Number _____

Product	Quantity	Sub Total	Total inc. £3.00 p.&p.
Geoff Hamilton 3D Garden Designer Version 3			
Geoff Hamilton Plant Encyclopedia			

I enclose a crossed cheque/ Postal Order made payable to GSP Ltd for:
£_____

Or please debit my [ ] Switch [ ] Mastercard [ ] Visa

Card No:_____ Valid From:_____

Issue No:_____ Expires: _____

Signature:_____

Rights and Restrictions: Offer available to UK residents only and closes on 25/12/04. Please allow up to 28 days for delivery. GSP (or via its agents) may wish to e-mail or telephone you with relevant offers for marketing purposes. We may also share information with relevant third parties. Please tick the box if you do not want to be contacted by us [ ] or third parties [ ] for these purposes.

REF GSP Creative Gardening with a Computer for the Older Generation